DESKBOOK OF
EXECUTIVE EXCELLENCE
AND
STRESS MANAGEMENT

Skills, Tactics, & Tips for
Superior Job Performance

DESKBOOK OF
EXECUTIVE EXCELLENCE
AND
STRESS MANAGEMENT

Skills, Tactics, & Tips for
Superior Job Performance

Designed for
Executives, Managers,
Doctors, Lawyers, & Engineers

S. A. SWAMI, Ph.D.

A MINIBOOK CLASSIC

Minibook Publishing Co.
Montgomery, WV

Copyright 1993 by S. A. Swami
Published by Minibook Publishing Co.

This publication is designed to provide accurate and authoritative information in regard to the subject matter covered. It is sold with the understanding that the publisher is not engaged in rendering legal, accounting, or other professional service. If legal advice or other expert assistance is required, the services of a competent professional person should be sought.

Library of Congress Cataloging-in-Publication Data

Swami, S. A. (Shanmugam A.), 1928–
    Deskbook of executive excellence and stress management : skills, tactics, & tips for superior job performance : designed for executives, managers, doctors, lawyers, & engineers / S. A. Swami.
        p.   cm.
    "A Minibook classic."
    Includes bibliographical references and index.
    ISBN 0-941553-02-7
    1. Executive ability—Psychological aspects. 2. Executives—Psychology. 3. Stress management. I. Title.
    HD38.2.S93   1993
    658.4'09—dc20   92-8055
                                                                    CIP

To

Saraswathi, Lakshmi, & Parvathi

ACKNOWLEDGMENTS

I would like to thank the Purdue Research foundation, Purdue University, Lafayette, Indiana, for the use of the Purdue Rating Scale for Administrators and Executives.

It is my pleasure to thank George Davis, President, and Linda Aguilar, Personnel Director, Merchants National Bank, Montgomery, WV for making available their personnel evaluation procedures for review and research.

I would like to extend my thanks to Julia Brown for her valuable assistance in copy-editing and comments during the manuscript preparation.

The assistance provided by my wife Anusuya Swami and our son Jay in the various phases of this book project is greatly appreciated.

CONTENTS

Preface:

How This Book Was Written and Why

PREFACE

HOW THIS BOOK WAS WRITTEN & WHY

Effective performance is required of all executives, managers, and professionals in their respective positions. Performance is a function of knowledge and skill, judiciously applied to the job or jobs on hand. However, a superior performance calls for something more than these; it needs a touch of personal desire and motivation to excel. It also needs a synergistic combination of a knowledge of principles, skills, and tactics pertaining to the field of operation.

It is the primary aim of this book to give the reader a complete but concise package of principles, skills, tips, and tactics for continuously effective performance required of executives and professionals. It has been my observation that superior performance of executives and professionals occurs because of their willingness to walk that extra mile and their ability to motivate and move with the team, assuming that they have the basic functional skills.

Searching for a better method of identifying the conventional executive skills for self-evaluation and self-development yielded the following grouping of the various skills: R-Skills (Reinforcer skills),

M/A-Skills (Management/Administrative Skills), and S-Skills (Synergistic Skills). They are presented in that order to give a total spectrum of what is needed for superior performance for the executive.

The salient feature of this book is Chapter 7 on the Executive Principles propounded by Thiruvalluvar, 3rd century BC philosopher, poet, and saint of India, translated from the original called "Thirukural" written in Tamil. The executive audience of the western world, though exposed to the ideas of Confucius of China and Machiavelli of Italy, is totally unaware of the wisdom of Thiruvalluvar. To bring to executive focus for the first time the precision and depth of insight of Thiruvalluvar principles is one of my primary considerations in writing this book. I have tried to present the original as unaltered as possible except for possible flaws in my translation.

Ability to manage stress and maintain good physical health is no longer considered as a secondary skill for executives and professionals; it is vitally needed for their career success and achievements to take them through the rigors of the competitive career life. The basic principles of dealing with stress and health are presented in Chapters 8 and 9 respectively.

The book is ideally suited for the young executive who steps into the career world, to MBA and MGA students pursuing executive careers, and to all executives, managers, and administrators at all levels. Every professional is an executive in one way or another, and the book is so designed to suit the needs of all professionals from the principles, skills, stress, and health points of view for superior performance.

Montgomery, WV   S. A. Swami
January 1, 1993

PART 1

PSYCHOLOGICAL FACTORS

CHAPTER 1

EXECUTIVE PSYCHOLOGY

"The executive is one who is knowledgeable on the instruments, ways and means, the time for action, the course of action, and the difficulties on the way to achieve success in the enterprises undertaken."

Thiruvalluvar
3rd century B.C. philosopher, poet, and saint of India, author of Thirukural, (verse 631)

TOPICS

Who is an Executive?
Nature of the Executive's job
What is Executive Psychology
Principle of Role Playing
3 in 1 Personality
Core-self
Functional-self
Career-self
Male/Female Executives
Self-Psychoanalysis

WHO IS AN EXECUTIVE?

It is generally defined that an executive is a person or group having administrative or managerial authority in an organization, which may be a company, corporation, bank, hospital, Foundation, college, university, etc. The chief officer of a government, state, or political division is also commonly recognized as an executive. The administrative or managerial responsibility includes **planning** for the effective functioning, growth, and profitability of the organization, **decision making** on issues that influence or affect the organization, **leading** the organization towards its objectives and goals and **creating** a healthy environment and opportunities for development and career growth for the employees at all levels.

From a functional point of view a pyramid structure for the employees of an organization has been found to be the most effective and is the basis of organizational set-up for small and large companies, corporations, and government departments in the United States of America. At the lower and middle level of the pyramid the persons responsible for the effective functioning of the units of the organization, though called upon to bear some degree of managerial and administrative responsibility to their division or department, are not called executives. Often they are designated as managers, foremen, department heads, etc. The persons serving at the top level of the organizational pyramid are generally referred to as executives.

However, there is no universal agreement as to who an executive is. The widely accepted notion is that an executive is one who carries out his/her job responsibilities through appropriate delegation and management of the resources and people who report to him/her. In this sense, an executive may be considered as one who gets things done through other people as well as himself/herself. What distinguishes an executive from an employee is the former's role in planning, decision making, and providing leadership for the growth and profitability of the organization, whereas an employee has no such input in its functioning.

NATURE OF THE EXECUTIVE'S JOB

The primary responsibility of an executive is to initiate and carry out such actions needed to achieve the goals of the organization through proper management and administration. However, not all executives are directly involved in all aspects of the administrative and management functions. The complexity and size of an organization determine the number of executives and the nature of their job function. An executive in a small organization generally holds many different functions, whereas in a large organization executives may hold specialized job functions such as administration, accounting, design, production, marketing, advertising, sales, etc.

The important point to note here is that no two executives may have identical job functions, and each executive position is unique in one way or other. Accordingly the skills needed for effective executive performance are also different. Apart from technical and professional skills such as engineering or accounting which needs specialized education and training, there are many other skills and characteristics which all executives need to possess. These are not generally taught in schools and colleges in a formal sense. It is the objective of this book to fill this gap and make the executive become aware of the need for continuous self-development in many areas which may have a direct bearing on his/her performance and success in carrying out his/her job functions.

WHAT IS EXECUTIVE PSYCHOLOGY?

Executives are not an exclusive class of people who are totally different from the rest of humanity. They are men and women coming from the same society which also provides other professionals and non-professionals for the career world. The difference lies in the job function only. Executive psychology deals with all the pertinent aspects of behavioral and educational psychology applicable to the executive in carrying out his/her administrative and/or managerial functions. It emphasizes the need for attitudinal and behavioral modifications on the part of the executive to suit his/her job functions for better performance. It also defines the subjective skills needed for executive achievements and to safeguard oneself from maneuvering from others in a competitive corporate environment.

PRINCIPLE OF ROLE PLAYING

Role playing is an important concept in human behavioral psychology. Necessarily, knowingly or unknowingly, a person plays many different roles in the course of his/her daily life such as being the son/ daughter to one's parents, father/mother to one's children within the fold of family environment. At the office or place of work the same person may work as a teacher, salesperson, executive, nurse, physician, policeman, etc. The professional person is not different from the family person; nevertheless, the person's behavioral interaction with others is dependent on his being aware of this distinction between the roles he/she is playing each time.

From this view point, it may be seen that a person working as an executive, male or female, is only playing a professional role and that he/she is expected to play the role to the highest degree of efficiency. However, due to differences in the human individuality different persons function differently in their role as an executive. Though there is no standard yardstick to measure the relative performance of executives, literally every executive is evaluated in some form or other in every organization. It is important to realize that the executive is evaluated at the functional level for his/her competence in carrying out responsibilities.

The critical factor underlying role playing for a person is the difference in responsibility associated with the role. It is obvious that the responsibilities of a father or mother at home for a person is drastically different from that of being an executive at his/her office. Whenever the role player is conscious of the responsibilities and the role, he/she can be expected to do a better job at the role playing. The roles may be many but the person is the same. Who is this "person"?

CONCEPT OF 3 IN 1 PERSONALITY

From a psychological point of view, a person is considered to have a mind of his/her own. The complexity of the notion of this mind itself is beyond normal human comprehension. It is the aim of behavioral psychology to unravel the mystery of the mind to some degree so that the factors influencing individual human behavior can not only be understood but also used for desirable behavioral modifications.

The word 'personality' is often used to denote the overall characteristics or traits of a person. However, from a career or professional point of view it is totally inadequate for meaningful communication to describe or explain the person's responses in the career environment. From our focus on executive performance in role playing, a person may be considered for all practical purposes as three different 'self' rolled into one:

a core self,
a functional self, and
a career self.

Though academically inclined psychologists may raise their eye brows at this trichotomy of the self, it has ample merit from a pragmatic point of view for subjective self-improvement for the executive.

CORE SELF

The core of a person is the human individuality derived from whatever constitutes his/her psychological make-up. It is not amenable for analysis objectively. However, subjectively a person can have some insight into his/her own core self through meditation and self-psychoanalysis. What we normally recognize as the core person is through his/her **unique** likes, dislikes, value system and behavioral characteristics. It is this uniqueness that gives the person his/her individuality. The core reflects the genetic and psychological potentials giving the person the identity and uniqueness that he/she is.

FUNCTIONAL SELF

Functional self refers to that aspect of the personality which embodies functional characteristics. What exactly are functional characteristics? These are the characteristics that are unique to the person, perceptible in his/her actions and dealings with other people. They are capable of creating impressions of the person in the minds of others, such as a lazy, or busy, or loving, or a patient person. It is an inexplicable combination of what psychologists call "personality traits". Though some of them are partly innate, most are learned or acquired through past experiences as adaptation responses.

It is important to realize that functional characteristics are "learnable" or "acquirable", thereby improving the functional self. Apart from their power to create impressions and images in the minds of other people, functional characteristics form the basis for performance in any career.

Functional Characteristics

Following are the basic functional characteristics which are culti-
vable. Besides, they are contributory to effective performance in any
career:

Honesty
Love for work
Enthusiasm
Punctuality
Reliability
Patience
Amiability
Adaptability
Morality

It must be noted that most of these characteristics can not be
compartmentalized and construed as independent entities, because
many of them overlap on each other. However, since they have their
origin in the value system of the individual, these characteristics are
extremely meaningful in the realm of interpersonal relations.

It is essential to realize that functional characteristics constitute
your "personality make-up" and they can not be faked. But you can
consciously improve on them to bring about self-improvement.

Honesty

It may appear too commonplace to tell a career person about the
need for honesty; yet, we have to emphasize that career activities, for
that matter of fact all civilized social interactions in any walk of life,
are based on the fundamental premise of honesty. To establish yourself
as an honest person is a prerequisite for getting started in your career.
Honesty is being without wilful deceit or fraud and implies sincerity.
Establishing a reputation for honesty is a continuous process through
words and deeds.

Love for Work

It is often argued that people will work only if they have to work.
Of course, it depends on what that work is about. However, it is a
psychological trait in humans to apply themselves to something or
other which interests them because the mind is always active. From a

career point of view, people with love for work certainly enjoy what they do; they also perform better than those who don't have the natural inclination to work.

Enthusiasm

Enthusiasm is nothing else but a keen and active interest with which a person applies himself/herself to any activity. The point to note is that it is this element of interest that kindles a sense of joy or happiness at the emotional level, thereby making the activity into a source of pleasure for that person. It does not matter what that activity is. Some people seem enthusiastic in everything they do, whereas some others show enthusiasm only in a few things. Enthusiasm holds the key to success in personal and career matters.

Punctuality

A sense of being punctual or otherwise is a personality trait and it emanates from the value system a person has evolved into. The degree of importance one attaches to being punctual is a very personal matter. Church meetings and family dinners are pretty much indicative of the importance he/she carries towards a sense of time when other people are involved.

From a career point of view the importance of punctuality can not be overstated. As a deficient functional characteristic it can be highly detrimental to career advancement. On the other hand, a functionally punctual person does create an impression of responsibility when others and their time are concerned.

Reliability

The single most important question that generally runs through the minds of interviewers and employers is "Is this person reliable?". Of course, it has nothing to do with your college degree which only tells them that you have undergone the necessary academic training that may be needed for the job. It is important that you realize this simple fact that reliability is a functional characteristic of an individual which is rooted in the person's value-system. It is considered as one of the personality traits.

Your future career success depends on the reputation of reliability that you have built around you through your activities and assignments slowly and steadily. It plays an important role in all teamwork and leadership situations.

Patience

Patience is undoubtedly one of the cardinal virtues that anyone can develop which can make a world of difference in personal and career life. Patience is uncomplaining in matters of normal social interactions where things may or may not go according to one's liking and expectations. It indicates an ability to tolerate others' shortcomings: it also is a sign of maturity in worldly matters. It is a functional characteristic of an individual easily visible to others. Though patience is generally beneficial to the practitioner in many ways, its impact is most felt in the area of stress management. A person with a patient disposition is less affected psychosomatically than a highstrung impatient person.

From a career point of view, patience as a functional characteristic is a necessity for building a successful career. The interpersonal relationship of a patient person is not only superior to that of an impatient counterpart, it also wins more friends for that person in the long run in any kind of career environment. Any thing worthy of achievement needs patience.

Amiability

Amiability is a friendly or pleasing disposition. Of course, such a disposition can not be faked. It emanates from the psychological make-up of the person imbibing all of the foregoing functional characteristics. Since amiable people are easy to get along, they find their place easily in social and career situations.

Though for some amiability may seem to be innate and natural, for others it can be developed or cultivated at the conscious level to a reasonable degree.

Adaptability

Flexibility in personal approaches to real world problems without sacrificing principles, legal, moral or ethical, is a functional characteristic of great pragmatic significance. To develop this characteristic one must be aware of his/her values, attitudes, and goals in life and be willing to openness and continuous learning. People with dogmatic ideas and rigid attitudes find it hard to adapt to changes around them. They seldom realize that their attitudes towards themselves, others, and the world they live in need constant reviews subjectively. The are quick to blame everyone else but themselves when things go wrong.

From a career point of view, personal adaptability is not only highly desirable but is also needed for successful management in complex situations.

Morality

Morality, in fact, is concerned with virtuous conduct with what is right and what is wrong. A moral person has respect for law, order, and ethics; and as such it can be asserted that morality as a functional characteristic is a highly desirable personal quality. Also, the social and economic stability of a nation is dependent on the morality of its citizens. Many social problems are directly indicative of the lack of sensitivity to morality as a functional characteristic on the part of its members.

From a career point of view, a career without morality is unthinkable. It is expected that every career person builds his or her career ethics on a personal sense of morality, which, of course, is a functional characteristic. You have to remember that a college degree and career skills by themselves do not make a person moral. It is where an uncorrupted value-system and positive attitudes are needed on the part of the executive at the psychological level.

CAREER-SELF

Career-self is that part of the personality that is tuned for the planning, preparation, and performance in a chosen career. It encompasses the functional and core aspects of the self. It may be visualized as a mantle wrapped over the functional and core personality. A person can totally change the career part of the self, but yet the underlying self remains the same in its functional and core characteristics. **The secret of executive excellence lies in the tuning of not just the career-self but the functional- and core-self as well.**

To be successful as an executive a person must develop the career self to its fullest potential. It is the objective of this book to present the skills and capabilities needed for top level performance for the executive in his/her career environment, so that the career-self can be developed to its performing best.

We want to emphasize the fact that the career-self does not have an independent existence of its own. A person in any career may be considered as a 3 in 1 personality only in a Gestalt sense for the purpose of delineating certain aspects of the human personality for an understanding of his/her job performance.

MALE/FEMALE EXECUTIVES

The concept of core plus functional plus career self is equally valid for both male and female executives. The development of skills and capabilities for top performance as an executive is a matter of individual motivation.

SELF-PSYCHOANALYSIS

No executive can excel without self-motivation. Fortunately, the desire to excel is an inborn nature in human beings. Though the innate instinct for excellence is a powerful motivator for many of his actions at the subconscious level of his mind, man is the only being in the animal world who can consciously induce in himself motivations and, thereby, pursue a life of excellence. Motivation may have its origin in intellectual stimulation and curiosity about the phenomenal world, or it may arise from **the desire to achieve in the competitive world.**

Self-psychoanalysis is an effective technique for the executive to have a glimpse at his/her own mental make-up, values, and attitudes, which can be effectively used to motivate himself/herself in the career life by choosing a suitable career path.

CHAPTER 2

FACTORS PREVENTING EXECUTIVE EXCELLENCE

"There are things that ought not to be done and if you do them you will be ruined; and there are things that ought to be done and if you don't do them you will be ruined also."

Thiruvalluvar,
Thirukural, (verse 466)

TOPICS

Lack of Purpose in Life
Lack of Positive Self-Image
Lack of Motivation, Will, and Discipline
Procrastination and Laziness
Lack of Patience
Lack of Humanistic Sensitivity
Emotional Turbidity
Cognitive Distortion

LACK OF PURPOSE IN LIFE

Have you ever asked yourself "What is the purpose of my life"? It is not often that people ask themselves the question of purpose in their lives. Many are not even aware that there can be a purpose in their lives. There is no dearth for cynics who scoff at the idea that there can be purpose in anybody's life. Yet, the truth of the matter is that not only there is purpose in everybody's life but also that one's life becomes more meaningful when that person becomes aware of that purpose.

Purpose is a specific objective or goal or goals worth striving for in a person's life. When you become aware of this fact, you will begin to see your life from a different perspective leading to a life of success and fulfillment. The logical question then is who assigns the purpose. The answer, of course, is you! Once you assign yourself one or many goals in your life, the hidden potential for self-excellence in you aligns your thought process and actions towards their fulfillment. On the other hand, lack of purpose simply lets you drift in life without any specific direction; your life energy gets wasted in reacting to the daily chores of routine living. Your dormant potential for excellence can not be awakened under these circumstances.

LACK OF POSITIVE SELF-IMAGE

Self-image is a nebulous concept hard to express and communicate in words. It is the way in which a person perceives himself/herself subjectively at conscious and subconscious levels. This self-perception is molded basically on the emotional experiences of the past and the socio-cultural upbringing of the individual. The self-image plays a key role in all human behavior and endeavors.

When the self-image is positive the person will be able to put forth a positive interaction with the outside world. Also, he/she will be self-confident in his/her decisions and actions. On the other hand, a person with a negative self-image displays a poor or low self-confidence, making him or her unsuitable for any competitive environment. Positive self-image and self-respect go hand-in-glove. Executive excellence is a myth for a person holding a poor esteem of himself/herself.

Fortunately, self-image is not a fixed entity. It is amenable for improvement through new experiences and self-analysis. How to build a positive self-image is presented elsewhere in this book. Any executive in quest of excellence must build a positive self-image before he/she takes on the career path.

LACK OF MOTIVATION, WILL, AND DISCIPLINE

Few executives realize that the single most important ingredient to success in any project a person undertakes is a genuine desire emanating from the person himself/herself to get involved in the project. Incentives provided externally such as bonuses, promotions, and salary rises are no match for the self-induced desire to participate in the project. This desire is often referred to as motivation. Psychologically speaking, there are two inseparable elements in motivation—will and discipline.

Will

Will draws the line between success and failure. it is the foundation of all human achievements. It the lack of will that is the greatest stumbling block in front of your goals. Will is the determination to get the activities done which are necessary to achieve the goal. It is the will that makes you move against seemingly insurmountable obstacles.

Lack of will makes decisions and efforts meaningless. Many a person falls into the rut of mediocre living not because of lack of imagination, but because of a lack of will to act consistently towards high-set goals. The unfulfilled dreams of success and the unrealized goals stand as everlasting monuments in the life of an individual reminding him/her of his/her good intentions. It is legendary that the path to hell is paved with good intentions. The missing link is the human will. Where there is a will, there is a way—to achieve your goals.

Self-discipline

Self-discipline on the part of the individual constitutes the physical component of his/her motivation. Will and discipline are the two sides of the same coin; one implies the other. Will is non-manifestive, whereas discipline is manifestive; in simple terms, will shows up through self-discipline. Together they have the potential to take you towards any desired goal—materialistic or non-materialistic, physical or intellectual.

PROCRASTINATION & LAZINESS

Nothing in the human nature is more loathsome than laziness. Laziness must not be confused with rest and relaxation, which are beneficial to the body and mind. Being lazy is willfully wasting the precious life energy, which should be harnessed and used for the enrichment of your life. The greatest boon one can ask of is to be alive and healthy, and for this reason the wise consider being alive as a privilege and not a right. How right they are! A privilege should not be abused or misused. Being lazy is downright abuse of your privilege. Besides, laziness prevents your hidden potentials from flourishing since conscious effort during your waking hours is needed to unearth, nourish, and develop them.

Self-fulfillment and creative self-expression are totally not possible for the lazy person. Goal-setting and achieving, however humble the goal may be, is beyond the reach of the lazy. Success and laziness do not go together; oil and water do not mix.

Procrastination is the tendency to put off things for tomorrow which can be done today. It is partly rooted in laziness and partly in a lack of motivation. The impact of procrastination is unmistakable—poor grades for the student, missed deals for the executive, missed promotions and raises for the office worker, and piled-up household chores for the homemaker.

Getting motivated in the event that is being postponed is the key to solving this problem. However, it is up to the individual to reflect on the problem and find a means of motivation. With a positive mental attitude and a coordinated career and life plan there will be less room for procrastination when you become serious in managing your time effectively each day.

LACK OF PATIENCE

In a world of drive-in banks, fast-food restaurants, and instant "kicks", patience as a desirable characteristic seems to have been pushed to the back seat in the lives of many people. Yet, it is patience that is needed to wither the stresses and strains of a calamity that might strike anytime in a fast pace of moving.

Achievement of all things worthwhile in life requires effort and patience. Patience provides the capacity to endure all that is necessary in attaining a desired goal. It is the most valuable tool for the ambitious executive who has set many goals for himself/herself in career and personal life. Patience thwarts frustrations and reinforces the self-possession needed in confronting obstacles and delays. Further it helps to manage career and personal stresses effectively.

Patience is the foundation of all other cardinal virtues, such as courage, charity, and tolerance. It is the basic fabric of self-excellence into which are woven all other positive mental attitudes. Positive self-image and executive excellence are myths without patience.

LACK OF HUMANISTIC SENSITIVITY

By the very nature of their job it is inevitable for the executives to come into contact with other people in their own as well as other organizations. Volumes have been written on the topic of interpersonal relationship and how to deal with others under varying situations from being firmly assertive to benignly negligent. Few executives realize that the very foundation of good interpersonal relations rests with the person himself/herself in the form of self-respect.

Self-respect

Self-respect implies the confidence in one's worth as a human being and a genuine concern to maintain it. It is also the basis for a positive self-image. Without it, effective interpersonal relations are not possible for any person. Frequently you hear people saying during the course of a casual conversation:

"I can never do things right"
"I always go wrong"
"I commit too many mistakes"
"I am hanging in there"
"I am not that good-looking."

These statements tell you indirectly how the person views himself/herself. The self-negation is subconsciously permeating the thinking process of the individual, and as a result he/she has such a poor self-image. You can anticipate these people having difficulties in managing their career and life problems.

Besides self-negation, a lack of healthy respect and appreciation for one's own achievements, however humble they may be, is a contributory factor to the poor self-image. Esteem and confidence build up by taking pride in your past successes and reflecting on them.

Respect for Others

Psychologists have recognized it as a basic need of human beings to desire for the acceptance, approval, and recognition from other people. How can you expect the respect of other people, if you don't respect them?

Looking at others as objects to be managed and manipulated is a popular notion in people management. A person nurturing this view may climb up a corporate ladder for a while, but soon find himself/ herself being managed and manipulated by others in the hierarchy often resulting in irreparable damage to his/her self-respect. Of all the sources of the woes of executive stress nothing is more perennial than the one that emanates from a lack of human sensitivity.

EMOTIONAL TURBIDITY

Emotional turbidity is the state of mind of a person when he/she flares up with emotional outburst even at a seemingly trivial incident, for example, a parent flaring up at a child for soiling his clothes at play. Oftentimes, the problem is subliminal; that is, the real cause of the emotional expression is at the back of the subconscious without the person being aware of it. The emotion clouds the reasoning, and the person tends to over-react compared to a normal and healthy reaction appropriate to the incident. Chances are that you might have seen this behavior in offices where bosses flare up, where peers snap at each other, and at home where the spouse cracks at the least provocative situation.

If you are guilty of this behavior, you need to "look-into" yourself and do some self-analysis to get out of this disorder. Seeking professional help is recommended for this malady. Emotional turbidity is the antithesis of equanimity of mind and prevents the development of a positive mental attitude towards others. It is an unmistakable sign of immaturity and a lack of inner growth, intellectually and emotionally. Some psychologists consider this as a distinct neurosis, a behavior disorder. The person displaying emotional turbidity is dubbed as "an infantile adult".

The person suffering from emotional turbidity usually ends up with a poor self-image and low self-esteem, because of his/her tendency to feel remorse and guilty after the emotional outburst. Frequent occurrences of emotional flare-up leave the person high-strung and nervous. It indicates that he/she is in a state of prolonged stress, which could make the person chronically and physically tired. Emotional turbidity is a clear symptom of a person who has not learned the art of emotion management.

COGNITIVE DISTORTION

Psychologically speaking, the formation of attitudes and value system for a person is a complex phenomenon. It is a continuous process starting from birth and it is often referred to as the secondary evolution for that person. A person's intellectual and emotional development and interactive experiences contribute to his/her perception of the world around him/her. It is this perception that plays a great role in the formation of his/her attitudes and behavior. When the perception is lop-sided, faulty, or biased his/her very attitudes and value-system in life can become deviant from those of others. It is nowhere more apparent than in the areas of money, sex, and success. Psychologists refer to this behavioral response as **cognitive distortion.**

It should be pointed out here that this is quite different from the situation where one feels an internal state of discomfort or conflict when one perceives inconsistencies between one's own attitudes or between one's attitudes and his/her own actions. This state is known as cognitive dissonance.

In cognitive distortion the person does not experience any conflict within himself/herself, but he/she clashes head-on with others with different perceptions about the issue involved. It becomes a stressor for him/her when the clash leads to friction in interpersonal relations.

Money

Money has occupied the center stage of many executives' lives and has taken such a grip on their thinking that it is hard for them to think of an event or action without associating a money value to it. Of course, money is important in the modern world but its due place in the process of living must be delineated by a reasonable and meaning-ful desire compatible with one's missions and goals in life without sacrificing the humane sensitivity. When an executive goes after money as if money is everything to live for, cognitive distortion alien-ates him/her from all human values. It becomes a neurosis in itself—an antithesis of executive excellence.

Sex

Attitudes towards sex has been undergoing transformation and there is no such thing as a standard notion on sex. However, a healthy attitude towards sex is of paramount importance because it involves the feelings of another person. Also, it is conditioned by the code of ethics and laws of the society where one lives. Any conflicting attitude has the potential to become a serious stressor.

Success

There is magic in the word "success", particularly in the modern materialistic environment which encourages competition literally in every aspect of our living from that of career to sports and relaxation. Proper and healthy attitude towards competition and achievement of success is very essential. "To become successful by hook or by crook" is undoubtedly a cognitive distortion on the part of the holder of this notion. As an ambitious executive desirous of becoming suc-cessful in your missions and goals, you should self-evaluate your atti-tudes towards success and confine yourself within legal framework in formulating your strategies. Unrealistic goals and employing improper means are nothing else but cognitive distortions.

PART 2

SKILLS, TACTICS, TIPS, & PRINCIPLES

CHAPTER 3

R-SKILLS
(REINFORCER SKILLS)

"Let him alone be selected for service who is well endowed with kindness, intelligence, capacity to make decisions, and who is free from greed."

Thiruvalluvar,
Thirukural (verse 513)

TOPICS

1. What are Reinforcer Skills?
2. Memory Power
3. Daily Planning and Review
4. Organization
5. Personal Time Management
6. Personal Finance Management
7. Interpersonal Relations
8. Dress to Impress
9. Socialization
10. Personal Hobby
11. Relaxation at Will

WHAT ARE REINFORCER SKILLS?

Reinforcer skills are those basic skills which are required for all people for efficient functioning at the personal level in career situations, and without which an executive can not perform effectively. No matter what career one pursues, these skills reinforce the efficacy of career skills one has acquired by virtue of education, training, and or experience. Reinforcer skills are not "taught" in a formal sense in schools and colleges as the career skills of accounting, engineering, etc.

R-skills are self-learned and practiced. They have the potential to streamline one's approach to life making it a source of pleasure and fulfillment. The so-called creative living has its foundation on R-skills. The following analogy serves to highlight the role of R-skills. In the same way as steel bars reinforce cement concrete in carrying heavy loads under varying stressing situations, R-skills serve as reinforcers to the professional/career skills of an executive.

Their greatest benefit lies in their ability to defuse stress in daily living. Their role in preventive stress management for the executive is discussed elsewhere in this book.

MEMORY POWER

A good memory is a great asset for the executive aspiring for success and professional growth. His/her performance on the job depends on it. Is a good memory Nature's gift to a few? Educational psychologists do not think so. They assert that all normal human beings are endowed with the same brain power and it is for the individual to learn the ways and means of keeping the memory in a sharp state.

Memory is the ability to recall events, information about previous experiences, or what has been learned before—a few minutes ago or many years ago. Memory of an event involves four phases: experiencing, storage, retaining, and retrieval. In short, to remember is to reinstate what has been previously learned.

Forgetting is the loss of the ability to remember and recall. It is considered to occur primarily due to the decay of the memory trace over time in the brain and to some extent due to the interference from other experiences. Absence of recall of the stored information over a long period of time seems to be the primary cause of forgetting for most people. Organic causes can also compound the forgetting.

How to Improve Your Memory

The secret of improving the memory lies in the frequency of recall process. Any experience or information to remain unforgotten must be reviewed mentally or through the appropriate senses of seeing, hearing, tasting, touching, and smelling many times in a day in the beginning and less frequently later till it becomes part of the long-term memory. Build a systematic recall session of the events, activities, and other desired information and include it in your daily schedule. Putting them in writing in a private log-book for review purposes is an excellent technique of remembering many things needed for your efficient performance.

Believe it or not, there is no other better technique to improve your long-term memory! In educational psychology this technique is known as "overlearning". Almost all accomplished musicians, artists, surgeons, educators, and other skilled people keep overlearning to maintain their top level of performance.

DAILY PLANNING & REVIEW (DPR)

Daily Planning & Review is more than a personal skill; it is a powerful habit. Like any other skill it can be learned and practiced by anyone. In fact, DPR has the potential to place an executive on course in goal-oriented missions—in personal and professional life, no matter what walk of life he/she is in.

The Technique:

1. Start the day with a planning session of about 5 to 10 minutes. List all the activities that are planned for the day on a piece of paper, and hold it right in front of you on your table.
2. Prioritize the activities depending on their relative significance and time factor, for example mailing a letter, contacting on phone, attending a meeting etc. Relist them in the prioritized manner. This is your guiding light for the day.

3. Get into the habit of glancing at this list every now and then. The list literally serves as a catalyst to kindle your action potential for optimum use of your time.
4. Cross out the activities as they are completed.
5. End the day with a 5 to 10 minute review session with yourself. Meditate over the finished and unfinished activities planned for the day to provide continuity for the next day of activities.
6. Carry over the unfinished activities, if any, for the next day. Remember that the review is not a mechanical stock-taking of completed and incomplete tasks. Its purpose is to ruminate over the why, how, and what of the uncompleted tasks besides to provide an efficient follow up and assessment of the completed ones.

The review session provides the chance for being ready for the next day for any anticipated difficult tasks. Nothing can improve the efficiency of the executive more than the skill and habit of going through DPR as a part of his/her time management.

ORGANIZATION

Organization plays such an important role in today's business world at every stage of administration and management that no ambitious executive can afford to overlook the skill of organizing in personal and professional spheres of his/her life. To organize is to systematize for efficient functioning. skill at organizing is personal life is a prelude to the ability to organize in the career and business world.

At the personal level anything from the organization of one's wardrobe to personal financial matters are all indicative of one's skill at organization. Since the career world is an extension of the personal world for an executive, developing the skill at organization is of paramount importance.

Unlike other skills, organization is rooted in the value-system of the individual at the psychological level, and as such it is essential to realize this fact before trying to develop it as a skill.

The Technique

The following steps will help to get better organized in personal life.

1. Carry put a self-evaluation of your attitudes (psychological aspect) and habits (mechanical or physical aspect) in personal life such as how you keep your study area, wardrobe, your room, your bed after getting up, kitchen sink, personal documents of all kinds, things in your car, etc.
2. If you don't take any particular care about them and have an attitude of indifference when they are strewn around in a jumble, you need to realize that functionally your skill at organizing is at its lowest ebb. Missing items, disorderly way of leaving things around, not being able to locate when you need an item or a document are but the tell-tale symptoms of a disorganized person.
3. Resolve to become better organized in all aspects of your personal life, particularly in those areas which you know that you are not well organized. This resolution acts as an auto-suggestion for you, goading you to adopt a behavior modification to break the old habit of disorganization. Remember that this resolution must emanate from yourself.
4. When you apply this technique to different facets of your personal life, you will find yourself emerging as a better-organized person. You will also realize that you will shape up better functionally, miss fewer things around your home, and manage your personal finances and bank accounts better.

PERSONAL TIME MANAGEMENT

Not many people think of personal time management as a personal skill to be developed to a degree of greater and better utilization of one's important natural resource. Time is something that they take for granted, seldom realizing that the kind of happy living they desire and dream about is dependent on their ability to manage their personal time.

Time Conversion (TC)

The skill of personal time management lies in the subjective realization of the concept of Time Conversion (TC).

TC is the process of initiating and carrying out an activity for a known duration of time towards a desired goal or result. It is the action part that leads to results. It is important to realize that it is not time per se that leads to results, but the activity undertaken during the time. Inaction (non-acting) is also an action in this sense.

As an example, let us say that you have an hour at your disposal, and that you have a television available. But your desire is to have an apple pie made. If you spend your time in the action of baking a pie your desire will be met with. Instead, if you chose to watch your favorite program on the television during this time, you desire to have an apple pie will simply remain a dream. It is the right action at the right time on your part that leads to the desired result.

This is TC at its simplified form. In the course of daily living we, of course, are doing many time conversions without being conscious of it, such as 30 minutes of getting ready to go to work, 15 minutes of driving to work, etc. However, when you consciously apply this concept of TC to your personal available time, you will be able to get the most out of your living; your time management will be at its best.

The Technique

The following technique can be used to improve one's skill of personal time management.

1. Make a desire-list of items that you care for which can be had by action on your part (not what money can buy) such as to maintain good health, to enjoy reading a novel, to play musical instruments, to spend time with your spouse and family, etc.
2. Make a weekly time-schedule of your personal time available for time conversion, leaving your career time, dinner time, and sleeping time.
3. Schedule a time for physical exercise. jogging, etc. to serve your desire to maintain health. Similarly, schedule a time table for other activities to serve your desire list.
4. This is a planned conversion of your personal time on a weekly basis. Keep the regularity of this schedule, and the results will slowly but steadily accumulate to satisfy your desire list.

Personal time management, in fact, is a reflection of a person's will power and discipline. It is effective only when the person undertakes it himself/herself. Remember that nobody can manage someone else's time.

PERSONAL FINANCE MANAGEMENT

It may look odd to list personal finance management as a personal skill. No matter how it appears to a casual reader, managing personal finances is not as simple as it looks. It is a skill to be learned and practiced. Few people realize that just by earning "a lot" of money one does not automatically solve all his/her financial problems. They also don't realize that there are principles to understand and follow in the handling of money once it is legally earned.

A knowledge of these principles will not only help you make effective use of your money for present living, but also for future financial independence when you are older and retired from your career. Besides, the same principles are equally valid for many situations in organizational financial management. The seven principles of personal financial management are presented in detail elsewhere in this book.

INTERPERSONAL RELATIONS

Undoubtedly one of the most desirable skills for a person in modern living is to be able to relate comfortably with other people. It may be in one's own home, place of work, or elsewhere. However, the dynamics of interpersonal relations in human behavior is so complex that it can not be reduced to a mechanistic skill of interaction. The interaction involves an emotional component, subtle or obvious, which, in turn, can precipitate further emotional responses. The question then is: Are there ways and means of interacting with other people effectively and efficiently and at the same time preventing unpleasant outcome in the relationship? Behavior psychologists affirm that there are when the person adapts the following values as his/her code of behavior in dealing with people:

1. Caring
2. Speaking pleasantly
3. Listening

4. Showing gratitude and appreciation
5. Impartiality
6. Humbleness
7. Non-jealousy
8. Willingness to help others.

Caring

A smooth human relation is not possible between two persons or a group of people without the individuals showing a genuine concern for the others. Caring for the physical and mental well-being of the other person implies that you place the other person's interest ahead of yours. This giving-in on your part draws the other person closer to you. A law of return in the psychological plane seems to work which states that people are compelled to give what they get.

How do you expect someone to care for you and listen to you, whether it is in your own home or office, if you don't have a sense of care and respect for that person? The moment "I don't care" or "I don't give a damn" attitude sets in, the relationship is heading for trouble and becomes a source of stress.

Caring means forgiving the faults of the other person and accepting him/her as a whole for what he/she is. Acceptance provides the ideal climate for better interpersonal communication in the home or office and makes the other person more receptive to your ideas. It is worth remembering the underlying law of psychology in creating the favorable climate for interpersonal relations which states that people like to be recognized as they are.

Caring also means sharing. It implies that you are willing to share your knowledge and assets to a degree meaningful to the relationship and situation. In office relationships this factor will win you many friends among your peers and loyal support from subordinates. Without a sense of caring and sharing, all other interpersonal communication techniques are meaningless.

Pleasant Speaking

Speaking is more than an art. It is the most effective tool of interpersonal communication. What you say, how you say, where or to whom you say are at your discretion and as such you can exercise caution and control in making speaking your powerful alley.

To speak pleasantly is something you should develop as an executive which can bring you great rewards. Pleasant speaking is not from the lips, but emanates from the heart. It can not be faked as others can "sense" the communication and its spirit.

Pleasant speaking excludes harsh and unpleasant tones and words, talking ill of a person, and utterance of useless words which do not contribute to goodwill. Speaking can be developed as a skill of expression; when you look smilingly at the other person and utter your words in a pleasant tone of sincerity emanating from the heart, you have already won his/her goodwill and friendship.

Listening

Ability to listen is an index of emotional maturity of an individual. It is an alley to one's ability of pleasant speaking, and is a powerful tool in helping to establish effective communication between two or more people.

Listening with undivided attention and respect encourages the other person to open up his/her mind and talk freely and draws him/her to your side. Effective interpersonal relationship is hinged on the fact that all human beings like to talk to people who listen to them.

Showing Gratitude and Appreciation

One of the reinforcers of the skill of good interpersonal relationship for a person is his/her ability to appreciate when others do something for him/her, however small or trivial it may appear. It may be through a simple oral expression, or a hand-written note to say "Thank You". It can be buying a lunch, or giving a small gift, or a promotion and salary where warranted. Of course, it is important that the response of the giver should be in good taste and in proportion to the help received or the hard work of the person involved which deserved a meritorious reward. What is more important is the sincerity behind the appreciation and gratitude which acts as the reinforcer in interpersonal relations.

An executive who is intent on good interpersonal relations should be aware that a timely help and action on the part of an employee is invaluable and that it can not be measured in monetary terms. However, some form of appreciation in good taste must be shown.

On the other hand, people who are not appreciative of others' good deeds can seldom be expected to build a good rapport with the people with whom they live or work. An executive who has not developed the art of appreciation can not be successful in professional relationships.

Impartiality

It is human nature to like some people and dislike some other people even before we had any interactions with them. This natural bias arises at the subconscious of the mind which we may not even be aware of. Yet, at the conscious behavioral level we should learn to conduct ourselves unbiased towards people with whom we come into contact, be it at home, office, or elsewhere. Impartiality as a behavioral ethic is a powerful reinforcer of interpersonal relations.

When impartiality becomes conspicuous by its absence in people's behavior, one runs the risk of being accused of showing partiality towards individuals and/or groups. Of course, it is the very antithesis of good interpersonal relations. As an executive you must pay special attention to being impartial at all situations, home and office alike. Nothing can win you more friends than people seeing you as an impartial person.

Humbleness

Humbleness as a personal virtue has been extolled by all philosophies of the world for the simple reason that humility creates a congenial climate for human interactive behavior and smooth functioning of an orderly society. Though it is good for everyone to be humble, it is all the more important for people in position and power.

On the other end of the scale is arrogance. Its impact on interpersonal relations at whatever capacity is always damaging. An arrogant person may be tolerated by others for the sake of position or money, but under the cloak of tolerance builds up an utter disrespect and even hatred. Good interpersonal relationship is meaningless when arrogance prevails. Arrogance has been the cause of downfall for many a person, kings and executives like.

Humbleness is not a sign of weakness as some people may consider. In fact it requires courage and maturity to be humble in dealing with people.

Non-jealousy

Jealousy is a negative emotion; it is envious resentment arising from one's not being able to have something deeply desired but not attained or owned by somebody else. Jealousy is nothing else but subliminal anger which could not be directed towards the other person. When jealousy is nurtured for a long period of time, the unspent anger turns on the self on two fronts simultaneously—physical and mental. Insomnia, headaches, and inability to relax are some of the symptoms of jealousy at the physical level; at the mental level negative attitudes towards the target of jealousy could slowly develop. These negative attitudes prevent meaningful and pleasant interpersonal relations with the other person.

Of course, it is human to feel jealousy. But to let jealousy persist and to nurture it secretly is not only unwise but also cowardly. Acceptance of disappointment and showing respect for the target-person of jealousy will pave the way for better interpersonal relations. Believe it or not, that is the only sensible way to overcome the pangs of jealousy.

Willingness to Help Others

The skill of interpersonal relationship is hinged on the willingness to be of help to others in a meaningful way compatible to the relationship. This is the reason why extremely selfish people have more problems in personal relations with others, in home or office. From a survival point of view man is basically a selfish creature; but realizing that collective survival contributes to individual survival the degree of selfishness becomes less conspicuous in most people.

Besides, willingness to help others is, to some extent, latent in all of us—again as a survival mechanism. To the degree a person exercises this willingness to help others, his/her interpersonal relations improve. Altruism, a genuine dedication to other people, is, of course , a saintly trait which is capable of winning more friends than any other. It is important that as an executive you should be aware of the fact that this helping tendency is a strong reinforcer of interpersonal relations at the personal and professional levels.

DRESS TO IMPRESS

"The person is half; dress is the other half", asserts an eastern proverb. It is no coincidence that an unwritten dress code prevails in the business world of executives requiring them to dress well. Dressing well does not mean expensive or fashionable clothes to put on; it implies to wear clothes of appropriate nature suited for the office. It also implies proper grooming and choice of shoes.

A well-tailored dark or light suit and conservative shirt and tie with polished black or brown shoes are appropriate for men. A conservatively worn dress and jacket of dark or light color and well polished pumps with a moderate heel are appropriate for women; casual light jewelry that is not too conspicuous can be used.

Though dressing is a matter of personal choice, executives, male and female, should be aware of its impact in image making in the minds of those who come into contact with them. Well fitting clothes do impart a sense of respectability in social settings as much as they do in the office. Dressing as a skill can be developed when one becomes conscious of its impact in his/her business life-style.

SOCIALIZATION

Seldom people think of socialization as an activity of skill. One should first learn or be aware of the etiquettes and manners that are appropriate for the type of gathering. It is better to move around and meet as many people as possible if it is a large crowd. In small gatherings, one should go around and greet all the people and exchange pleasantries. One must be very careful with the drinks when it comes to alcohol, if it is served in one form or another. It is better to avoid it totally if one can on principles, but if it is not possible one should stick to a sensible previously decided limit.

The purpose behind socialization is to get to know more people and talk with them in an informal setting of leisure and relaxation, which otherwise may not be possible for most executives due to busy office schedules. This can lead to an expansion of one's business contacts. Socializing with old friends helps to reinforce the friendship.

Socialization is a potential relaxer for most people when one is comfortable at the art of meeting and conversing with new people. Country clubs, Rotary clubs, Bridge clubs, and the like provide enough opportunities for an executive to develop the art of socialization.

PERSONAL HOBBIES

Though hobbies are activities carried on for pleasure, few people realize the latent potential of hobbies in developing skill and mastery in the chosen activity besides their being a means to relaxation—physical and mental. Since a hobby is personally chosen based on one's innate inclinations, the individual can excel in it and become more knowledgeable in that activity and related matters such as photography, archery, painting, collections of items of interest, computer usage, playing music instruments, etc.

If the hobby activity is related to your career interest, the skill and knowledge are transferable from one to the other. Undoubtedly it is a plus for an executive to have additional knowledge acquired from his/her hobby which is related to his/her career situation.

The primary purpose of a hobby, though, is to bring relaxation to the hobbyist. When one loses interest in one hobby, of course, new hobbies can be chosen to keep one pleasantly occupied for any length of time that one wants to spend.

RELAXATION AT WILL

To be able to relax at will is a skill that is not easy to come by. One has to learn and practice it. It is a skill on a par with communication—everyone needs it. For the executive it is doubly beneficial. Knowing the techniques one can invoke instant relaxation under stressful situations in daily living at home as well as office. Therapeutically it has preventive potential to ward off some of the physical ailments that are the outcome of stressful living, particularly headaches and muscle cramps at different parts of the body.

Induced relaxation at will clears the clouding of the mind and promotes clear thinking for problem solving. It also helps to buy time in difficult decision making situations.

However, as a skill self-induced relaxation is not well understood by many executives who always appear to be on the edge. Though there are many methods for relaxation at will, the following techniques are relatively simple which can be learnt easily and practiced both at office and home.

1. Diaphragmatic deep-breathing
2. Coffee/Tea cup gazing
3. Body Awareness relaxation
4. 5-minute meditation
6. Yogarobic Relaxation.

These techniques are presented in detail elsewhere in this book. Needless to say that a knowledge of these techniques is an asset for the executive who can use them to his/her best advantage under stressful conditions.

CHAPTER 4

M/A-SKILLS (MANAGEMENT/ADMINISTRATIVE SKILLS)

"Entrust the project to the person who has the right knowledge and who is willing to undertake it, and not to one just because you like him."

Thiruvalluvar,
Thirukural (verse 515)

TOPICS

1. What are M/A-Skills?
2. Communication
3. Functional Planning
4. Goal-setting and Achieving
5. Decision Making
6. Problem Solving
7. Delegation
8. Working with People
9. Executive Time Management

WHAT ARE MANAGEMENT/ADMINISTRATIVE SKILLS?

These are the skills needed for all executives and managers whether they are in the top, middle, or low level in the hierarchy. Without these skills no one can survive in the executive ranks. Deficiency in these skills will be a marked handicap for one who aspires to move up in the managerial and administrative hierarchy.

The performance evaluation of an executive or manager revolves around these skills, whether evaluated by the boss above or by subordinates below. They are:

1. Communication
2. Functional planning
3. Goal-setting and achieving
4. Decision making
5. Problem solving
6. Delegation
7. Working with people
8. Executive Time Management

These skills are presented "on principles" in this chapter. Application of them in the real world, of course, is situational and it is for you to apply them diligently in your situation. You can continuously improve yourself through feedbacks related to your performance in the use of these skills.

COMMUNICATION

The skill at direct and indirect communication is one of the vital skills for success in the career world which no aspiring executive can afford to be without. Volumes have been written on the topic of executive communication which serves to emphasize its importance. It is rather presumptuous to tell anyone in general, an executive in particular, what exactly communication is. However, it is not uncommon that many executive failures have been found linked directly to the deficiency of their talent in the skill of communication. It is an ironical fact that every executive thinks that he/she is good at communications in his/her career milieu. The truth, of course, can only be assessed from those at the other end of the communication process.

What exactly is good communication?

In its simplest form communication is the process of transmitting a piece of information, idea, or objective to another person to whom it is intended in such a manner that there is no misunderstanding, confusion, or ill-feeling. Good communication can bring about the following benefits in any organizational environment:

1. It can eliminate doubts and distortion of the matter communicated.
2. It can save time, energy, and money.
3. It can create a healthy emotional climate with the organization.
4. It can increase the bondage of a team.
5. It can produce a respectable and strong image for the organization.

By the same token, bad communication can be expected to cause the opposite effect. This only underlines the importance of the power and need of good communication in any organization. To a large extent the success of an organization is dependent on the quality of its executive communication.

Effectiveness of the organizational communication must be viewed from two perspectives:

1. System communication, and
2. Personal (executive) communication.

System Communication

This refers to the structural form of communication within and outside of the organization. Advertising, promotion, relations with share holders, consumers, community, government, media, etc, fall within the realm of external communication. These are best handled through a specialized section of the organization who can provide centralized and coordinated communication such as a department of public relations.

The internal communication, on the other hand, flows in accordance with established lines of authority and structural boundaries. Media for formal and official communication may include memos, letters, telephones, bulletin boards, in-house publications, newsletters, and "electronic mail".

Grapevine

Besides this formal internal communication you should be aware of the fact that an unofficial and informal communication system exists superimposed on the formal network in every organization, large or small, commonly known as the grapevine. As an aspiring executive it will be to your advantage if you learn to handle grapevine information with discrimination not giving undue importance to it but at the same time not ignoring it.

Personal Communication: How to Become a Better Communicator

Communication skill, as many erroneously believe, is not dependent only on effective speaking. In fact, the three most important skills for effective communication in today's highly organized world, besides effective speaking, are:

1. Listening,
2. Writing, and
3. Running a meeting.

Listening

Successful executives and managers are invariably effective and sympathetic listeners. Attentive listening gives them time for comprehension, and at the same time wins the friendship of the speaker. Following are five basic rules for more effective listening:

- Be sincerely attentive to the speaker and do not fake listening.
- Show your emotions and feelings of sympathy through facial expressions.
- Do not show negative emotions of anger or distrust to the speaker.
- Encourage the speaker with eye contact and an alert posture.
- Tolerate silence and pauses of the speaker, giving him/her time to express the situation in his/her own words.

Writing

Writing as a managerial communication tool can not be overemphasized. As a learned skill, effective writing is a product of regular practice. Those who do not get the necessary writing practice in college are seriously handicapped when they step up to the managerial firing line. Five basic rules for good writing are:

- Keep your words simple.
- Express your idea with clarity.
- Write concisely and precisely.
- Be specific and to the point.
- Use words and phrases that have some punch.

Running a Meeting

Meetings have become an integral part of modern organizational life, whether corporate, governmental, professional or community service. They are convened for many reasons, such as to find facts, devise alternatives, formulate action plans, to vote on issues, to pass along information, etc.

In the career world, meetings occupy a good deal of a manager's and executive's time, and hence it is important that his/her time not be wasted in these meetings. Well-conducted meetings use the participants' time and talents efficiently and contribute positively to the organization's objectives. On the contrary, poorly conducted meetings are not only a direct waste of company resources, but also can foster ill-will among the participants. The final responsibility for the outcome of a meeting, its success or failure, rests with the person who chairs the meeting.

Robert Kreitner, author of "Management", lists the following principles for conducting successful meetings:

1. Make certain that a meeting is necessary.
2. Develop an agenda and send it out in advance.
3. Give careful consideration to special invitees to the meeting.
4. Give the meeting your full undivided attention.
5. Be well prepared. Anticipate questions and issues that may arise.
6. Ask the right questions to stimulate discussions. Encourage everyone to get involved.

7. Keep to the agenda. Don't allow members to wander off the subject.
8. Conclude the meeting on time by summarizing the highlights.
9. Distribute a set of accurate and detailed minutes to all members before the next meeting.

Self-Reminder Communication

It is almost impossible for an executive to remember all the various activities and appointments other than routines that are to be attended to during the day, week, or ahead. Every executive should work out a system to get reminded that most suits his/her needs and resources. The most common self-reminder communication techniques are:

1. Keep a so-called "To-do" list for the day/week right in front of you, placed on the desk, for continuous consultation.
2. Inform your secretary to remind you at the appropriate time. Make sure that she/he has her/his own calendar correctly marked.
3. Get into the habit of carrying a personal time-minder diary, and more important, get into the habit of consulting it and browsing through it often.
4. Mark on the desk or wall calendars of extended time, such as monthly, quarterly, half-yearly or yearly for follow-up reminders.
5. Use sticker-memos for high priority activities and appointments and stick them right on your desk-pad or even on the telephone.

Self-Motivator communication

Self-motivator communications are reminders of a different kind with a different purpose. They serve as psychological boosters or motivator for the executive. They are words of wisdom appropriate for the personality of the executive. They may be quotes of famous people or coined by yourself. They may be displayed on plaques placed on the table in front of you or placed on the walls for casual glancing. They may also be written in your personal executive notebook or log for browsing through once in the morning or at any time. To be most effective, they must be diligently chosen by you appropriate for the activities and projects you are currently concerned with.

Some typical self-motivator communications are:

- "Do it Now".
- "Smile and the world smiles with you".
- "There is no such thing as the future; eternity is Now".
- "Success lies not in never falling but in rising up every time you fall".
- "Honesty is the best policy".

FUNCTIONAL PLANNING

By the very nature of the job every executive will be involved in some form of planning for the organization's smooth and effective functioning for the present and future, growth of its activities compatible with its mission, and for the welfare of the people working for the organization. No matter what kind of planning you are involved in, the following factors govern all planning situations on principles:

1. Objective or primary goal
2. On-the-Way goals
3. Resources
4. Time frame
5. Location of activity
6. Activity itself.

Objective or Primary Goal

Functional planning revolves around an objective. Since an objective is something that is aimed at, it is essential that the executive has a clear-cut vision of the primary objective of the mission undertaken. It is not enough to have a vague idea but it must be clear, precise, and without ambiguity. For communication purposes the objective must be written in a statement form in one sentence conveying the same meaning to all readers.

On-the-Way Goals

On the way goals are a series of goals necessarily to be achieved which will lead to the primary goal. No where in the planning process does an executive's vision and experience play a more decisive role than in visualizing and establishing on-the-way goals. Many great missions have failed due to inadequacy or want of this vital step in the functional planning.

Resources

Resources may be considered as the very foundation of the planning process. Without adequate resources the planning has no meaning. Technical and non-technical manpower, appropriate equipments, materials, and continuous monetary support compatible to the mission undertaken are the resources that must be evaluated and included in the planning.

Time-Frame

Planning without a meaningful time-frame is no better than wishful thinking. The time factor can be critical in many phases of the mission which must be evaluated and given due allowance for. Allotting a time for each phase of the whole project must be based on estimates that are neither overly optimistic nor pessimistic.

Location and Activity

Choice of the location for the whole project or part of it is as critical as any other element in the planning. Geographic location, nature of the terrain, accessibility to existing transportation network, availability of labor, proximity to supply of raw materials, and the potential market are among the important factors to be analyzed during the functional planning process.

Activity

Thorough analysis of the overall project under planning and the various associated activities must be undertaken in the planning stage. A feasibility study of the project can prevent serious hardships, economic or otherwise, later.

GOAL SETTING AND ACHIEVING

Principles of Goal Setting

For a goal to be achievable, it must have three characteristics:

1. a well defined objective,
2. a measurable target, and
3. a specified time-frame.

Absence of any one of these will reduce the goal to the level of only a good intention. Intentions don't take anyone anywhere. Goals must not be too rigid either. They must be flexible enough to accommodate changes and modifications, but rigid enough to produce measurable results. Above all, goals must be realistic.

On the personal side two elements are necessary for the goals to be achievable:

1. faith in yourself and the goal, and
2. innate liking for the goal.

It is meaningless to work towards a goal that one does not have faith in or a goal that one has not developed a liking for. Further, as an executive you can not motivate and lead others towards goals of your organization if yourself do not have unshaken faith in the objective of the mission.

Principles of Achieving Goals

However small or large, simple or complex, a goal appears to be, achieving it possible through the application of the so-called "seven laws of success". Because these principles are universally applicable in all situations of goal-setting they are known as "laws". They are:

1. Keep the objective at sight
2. Keep studying more about the goal
3. Make adequate preparation
4. Act with concentration and enthusiasm
5. Be willing for due sacrifice
6. Do not mind others' opinions
7. Get continuous feedback and analyze.

Objective at Sight

Keeping the objective at the top level of your mind at all times during working towards a goal is the first and foremost thing to remember. It acts as a catalyst mobilizing your thoughts and actions and steering them towards your objective.

Study More about the Goal

The objective, well-implanted in your consciousness, should be followed by a continuing effort on your part to learn everything possible within your limitations about the goal you seek. This study helps to bring to light the nature of the road ahead, the impediments on the way, the pitfalls to be aware of, and above all, your own shortcomings relative to the goal.

Make Adequate Preparation

The next step is to make preparations on your part. This is, in effect, to get control over the prerequisites compatible to the objective and the goal. Many an executive has failed in their ventures, not for lack of hard work but because of overlooking the need to get the prerequisites mastered in the first place. With the prerequisites taken care of, only now you are actually ready to embark on the action part of the goal-seeking mission, and you need an action plan.

An action plan is a well-conceived and thought-about step-by-step procedure to be carried out on daily, weekly, and monthly basis compatible to the time-frame of the project.

Act with Concentration and Enthusiasm

Remember that it is action that produces results. It is synonymous with work. Motivated, consistent, and systematic work according to the action plan is what you need now. It should not be the kind of drudgery of the sullen workaholic, but the exuberance of an enthusiastic executive. Besides enthusiasm, the secret of getting better results lies in the degree of concentration with which you apply yourself to the action part. Concentration is a true saver of time and energy.

Be Willing for due Sacrifice

It is inevitable that a certain amount of sacrifice of your personal time and comforts is called upon in the achievement of any worthwhile goal. There is no compromise on this fact. However, an enthusiastic goal-seeker does not consider it as a sacrifice because for him/her it becomes a way of life—not thrust upon, but willingly adopted. One thing you should guard yourself against is the undue infringement of your professional involvements into the harmony of your family and personal life. No professional success is worth the effort if it leads to alienation of a loving spouse and children.

Do not Mind Others' Opinions

While the opinions of others whom you live and work with do count, you should not pay attention to any discouraging or distracting comments about your goal. You should remember that a person's opinions are conditioned by his/her experience and limited by knowledge. Use your power of discrimination in weighing the opinions of others and never take them for granted. Do some investigation and research of your own before accepting or rejecting them. We mentioned before that your faith in yourself and in your objective is the seed of success, and you should learn to discount the opinions of others not founded on facts.

Get Continuous Feedback

Finally, getting continuing and periodic feedback about the results of your effort and the progress of the project undertaken on a measurable scale is a necessary condition for success. An evaluation of the feedback lets you know how well you are doing relative to your objective and the time-frame. It lets you decide to have changes and modifications in the approach and nature of execution, if needed. Periodic evaluation of the feedback serves as both a monitoring and warning device. It is a forerunner of what is yet to come. Its message is loud and clear for the goal-seeker, if you are tuned for it.

DECISION MAKING

It is inevitable that executives in management are under constant pressure to make decisions by virtue of the nature of their job. Decision making is a management function, and as such there is no room for shying away from it for managers and executives. Decisions are needed for simple day to day operations and productions in manufacturing processes; they are needed for selection of raw materials and supplies; they are also needed to hire and fire personnel, promote employees, give rises in salary and benefits, closing and expanding business wings; they are needed in negotiations and putting through complex business deals; they are also needed to outwit competitors.

Why Decision Making Can be Ordeal?

No matter what the issue is on which a decision is needed, the decision making is an ordeal to some degree for the decision maker if it involves a fear of failure. It is this fear of failure that lurks in the mind of every executive and prevents him/her from making an effective decision.

The underlying phenomenon, in fact, is not the issue calling for a decision; it is the self-image of the executive. Since the person tends to associate himself/herself with the outcome of the decision but is unwilling to accept the failure part of the decision, he/she thinks it is a reflection of his/her personality. The intensity of this conflict can be very high for persons with a weak self-image. On the other hand, persons with a stronger and more confident self-image are least affected by this conflict, even if it exists; because they have learnt to dissociate themselves from the outcome of their executive decisions.

Elements of Sound Decision Making

Decision making can be less traumatic and more objective when attention is paid to the following factors:

1. Purpose
2. Fairness
3. Evaluation of data
4. Anticipation of outcome
5. Openness to expert counseling
6. Willingness to take risk
7. Decisiveness.

It is imperative that the executive must be very clear in his/her mind about the purpose behind the issue calling for a decision. It is not uncommon to find executive failures of decisions based on misunderstood purposes. A sense of fairness must be exercised by the decision maker to all concerned, particularly if the decision involves people. It is inevitable that someone or many may be hurt or inconvenienced by decisions thrust on them over which they have no control in any free enterprise system.

A thorough collection and evaluation of data pertaining to the issue is a prerequisite for all decision making. Insufficient and improper data can be misleading; no decision can be considered sound based on them.

Decision making to a large extent is an introspective process balancing the above factors while anticipating the possible outcome. While it is not humanly possible to anticipate all the future ramifications of a decision, at least seemingly visible alternatives can be considered before the decision is made.

No executive can be an expert in all matters calling for his/her decision. It is a wise person who readily accepts self-limitations and pays heed to counseling from right quarters for a better decision making. It is essential to take a second expert opinion to be on the safe side in matters of great importance.

Decisions involve uncertainties of outcome and hence an element of risk to a smaller or larger degree must be considered as a part of decision making. The decision making executive must be willing to face this risk and try to minimize it in choosing alternate courses of action after the decision is made.

Finally, for a decision to be effective the decision maker must exercise decisiveness—the ability to be decisive. Once a decision is made he/she must stick to it following it up with appropriate actions planned for its implementation. Decisiveness also implies not feeling remorse or guilty and accepting the outcome with a sense of equanimity.

When Decisions Should not be Taken

Decisions made from a relaxed frame of mind are apt to be sounder than under the influence of emotions. When a person is in a state of emotion such as fear, anger, grief, or even joy, he/she can not rationally and objectively analyze issues on their merits and take appropriate decisions. He/she should defer taking decisions to a later time when the person is free from the emotional turbulence in the mind.

Decisions should not also be taken when the executive is under the influence of alcohol or drugs. Alcohol impairs judgment on a rational basis and one can not fully comprehend the implications and ramifications of the decision while the effect of alcohol is still lingering on the nervous system. All drugs other than those taken under medical supervision must be treated on a par with alcohol as far as their effect on decision making is concerned.

Deferment of Decisions

There are many situations in the business world which may warrant a delay in taking decisions. It is up to the executive to evaluate each situation on its own merit and take appropriate action of deciding or deferring. When conditions keep changing a deferment of a decision is better than jumping into one. Deferment is a temporary postponement of making a decision for a specific reason(s), and is not a solution to the problem. As soon as conditions stabilize a firm decision must be taken by the executive.

Procrastination in Decision Making

Procrastination is the action of willful postponement for tomorrow of what can be done today. Procrastination is deadly element in executive excellence and must be handled with care and caution. It is a reflection of a psychological insecurity arising from a weak self-image of the executive. It has its roots in an unwillingness to face the consequences of one's own decisions. No matter what the reasons are, procrastination in decision making almost invariably leads to loss and grief to the organization and the individual.

PROBLEM SOLVING

The skill of problem solving is nothing else but an organized analysis of a problem in its most logical sequence with a view to find the most appropriate solution. The first thing to do in problem solving is to delineate the problem in a clear statement and then to look at the factors precipitating the problem. In other words, by taking a gestalt look at the totality of the cause and effect relations leading to the problem it may often be possible to figure out the area requiring immediate attention for correction.

This principle is equally valid for problems dealing with materials as well as people. Of course, each problem is unique and it needs to be solved in the light of its contributing factors. Any solution imposed from outside without proper consideration of the underlying factors is most likely to fail.

DELEGATION

Need for Delegation

It is almost impossible for you as an executive to take upon yourself the performance of all the tasks associated with your job responsibilities all the time, however good or efficient you may be at work. The capacity of humans is limited, so is the time available for getting things done. When your responsibilities exceed your capacity to perform all the assignments yourself, you will be jeopardizing your own performance. The logical alternative is to let someone else within your authority such as your secretary, your assistants, subordinates, and others do some part of your work, so that you can get all work done required of your responsibility. This process is known in the business world as delegation.

However, delegation is not that simple and harmless as it sounds. It is a double-edged sword; it can work for you when properly done, or against you if it is not handled with care. The aim of delegation is to take some of the burden off your shoulder so that you can carry your own more effectively and perform efficiently.

Delegation as an Executive Function

Increasing your own efficiency is not the only reason for delegating a part of your job. Delegation is as much an executive function as planning or decision making. By enlargement of a subordinate's job through delegation you literally provide that person with an opportunity to enhance his/her worth to the organization. Delegation, per se, has the following potentials:

1. It can help develop his/her sense of responsibility.
2. It can enlarge his/her general understanding of the business part of the assigned tasks.
3. It can increase his/her job satisfaction by doing varied jobs of responsibilities.
4. In can enhance his/her self-image when he/she is able to carry out the added assignments satisfactorily.
5. Above all, delegation gives you as an executive a chance to develop your ability to pick up right persons for the right job (see Chapter 5) and build a team.

Types of Delegation

All delegations can be classified into three groups:

1. Function delegation
2. Assignment delegation
3. Authority delegation.

Function Delegation. This involves the delegation of one or more of the executive functions such as a short-term planning, which is normally expected to be done by the executive himself/herself. You must be extremely careful in delegating functions because it may reflect negatively on your capability as an executive. You should choose a person who is both capable and at the same time trustworthy.

Assignment Delegation. Any of your routine chores and any special assignments which do not require special skills can be assigned to your secretary and other subordinates.

Authority Delegation. Situations such as negotiations, hiring, representing the organization, etc., require a certain amount of authority. Delegation under such circumstances calls for care and diligence on your part to pick up a right person who can, not only carry the job, but also enjoys your confidence.

When to Delegate

You must realize as an executive that you can not and should not indiscriminately delegate your job responsibilities and tasks with a view to lighten your work. Such an action will boomerang with all its negative effect on you and can be deadly for your professional and career growth. The following situations are generally appropriate for delegation which you must weigh carefully before you decide.

1. **When you are away for a short period of time.** Your secretary or one of your subordinates can be entrusted to attend to your duties which are of routine or general nature and which do not require major decisions.
2. **When you are away for a long period of time.** Since decisions may be involved during a longer absence such as a vacation, you have to give your functional responsibility to someone who is capable of discharging those duties. Your chief assistant will be the most appropriate choice.

3. **Special Assignments.** Since these are not routine chores, you have to assign them to the right person who has the right skill or to one who has the potential to develop the skill needed for.

4. **Representing the organization.** To represent your organization in meetings and conferences, find someone who has not only the right qualifications but who is skilled at public relations with a polite behavior.

5. **Recruiting, Negotiations, etc.** These require not only specialized skills, but a deep understanding of human behavior and potentials. Mistakes committed in these activities can be costly to the organization, monetarily and reputation-wise. You have to exercise extreme caution in delegating these activities by choosing a trusted person who has proven loyalty to the organization.

When not to Delegate

Though delegating appears to be an easy way of handling executive duties, you have to be aware that not doing it right can land you in serious difficulties. The following are the key "don'ts" in delegating:

1. Do not let anyone else do any of your basic responsibilities which require technical skill. If you can find someone who has the skill, then make sure that he/she is trustworthy.

2. Never hand over the power to discipline to any other person however trustworthy he/she may be. It is the backbone of executive authority and must be safeguarded with care.

3. Never give the responsibility to maintain morale to others but you may call upon others to help carry out assignments that will improve morale.

4. Overall control, again, must be kept within your palms and never given to others however justifiable the situation may appear.

5. Duties involving trust and confidence must be kept by you, and it is better not to assign them to others.

How to Delegate

Delegation can be very effective when you adhere to the following guide lines:

1. **Instruct your delegate in depth.** Give your delegate a clear picture of what he/she is to do and how to do it. He/she must know the degree of authority you are investing in him/her. All information pertinent to the assignment, including with whom he/she is to deal and the possible difficulties he/she may face.

2. **Let others know and get them to cooperate.** It is essential to let all the people in your jurisdiction know publicly the limits of the authority you delegate. Without cooperation from others no delegation can be successful. Outline the importance of working harmoniously with all the members of your team. At the same time, you keep to yourself the right to discipline.

3. **Keep Control.** You must exercise control in order to achieve coordination—to make sure that the assigned task is in line with other objectives. You must keep control by suitable follow-up. Have your delegate report to you on how he/she is progressing on a periodic basis. Such a report may be written or oral, personal contact or over the telephone. It is for you to decide which is appropriate under the circumstances.

WORKING WITH PEOPLE

Personality Factors—"Know Thyself"

Elsewhere in this book we presented some of the basic principles of positive interpersonal relations with other people in general. The application of the principles, however, is a personal matter depending of the so-called "personality" of the individual.

As an executive you will be interacting with all kinds of people in different capacity and in different situations. Your effectiveness in dealing with them depends on your understanding of the dynamics of human behavior. To understand others, you must understand yourself first. The simple phrase "know thyself" has more meaning in a corporate environment than elsewhere. By placing yourself in the other person's shoes you can only partially comprehend the behavioral response under the job pressure because of the difference in your and the other person's personality factors.

Nevertheless, an attempt on your part to view things from the other person's point of view is the single most valuable tool you may have in working with people for greater effectiveness. Executive excellence is a myth if you can not reasonably comprehend the viewpoints of the people who constitute the corporate world.

Boss-Subordinate Relationship

All human relationships in the business, corporate, and governmental environment involve a boss-subordinate interaction in one form or another. The behavioral responses of individuals in this relationship is so delicate and complex that they defy any rational analysis. The psychological self-perception of the two individuals, boss and subordinate, and their value-systems and expectations constitute the basis of this relationship. They have the potential for being complimentary, and also for being contradictory. This is what leads to a harmonious relationship in some cases and to a friction-ridden relationship in others.

EXECUTIVE AS A SUBORDINATE

It is essential to remember that no matter what kind of person you are and what kind of person your superior is, you are still two different people: you have your own attitudes, your own way of doing things and so has your boss. An unless you know him/her well enough to be pretty sure of his/her views, standards, and approach to problems, you will be handicapped in your dealing with him/her.

Yet it is possible for you to bridge this gap to some degree by proper understanding. The way to understand your boss is through his/her words, actions, and decisions. The words a person speaks are indicative of not only his/her cultural disposition but also the attitudes. Attitudes, in fact, are the base or actions. By studying your boss's past activities and decisions, you can pretty much visualize a career-personality for him /her. It is this personality that you will be dealing with in the office environment.

The Tale of Two Egos

Central to all human behavior is the ego of the person. Between your boss and you, his/her ego and your ego are constantly facing each other through their respective attitudes and value systems. You aim should always be to avoid direct confrontation in your dealings but to go along with him/her without hurting your own ego. On matters of contradiction, you must make sure that you have all the facts in your favor and present them to the boss without hurting his/her ego.

Avoid Being an "Yes Person"

You should avoid being overly submissive or being an "Yes person" all the time trying to please your boss. This can hurt your self-image. When you know that the boss is wrong, let him/her know in a proper manner. The boss's ego may prevent him/her from acknowledging it at that instant, but his/her respect for you will keep increasing.

Avoid Being Hostile to the Boss

It is not uncommon to find an executive who tends to be overly aggressive toward his/her superior. His/her attitudes are such that he/she views the relationship as a constant cold war. For such an executive the boss is always wrong. Obviously, this is not only an undesirable way of dealing with superiors, but it is a highly detrimental path to the career growth of the executive.

Be Supportive of the Boss

In a hierarchial relationship harmony of the system is possible only when there is full support at every layer for those above. As much as the subordinate is expected to provide support to his/her boss, the later is expected to provide opportunities for the subordinates to grow and advance professionally and career-wise. It is often the clash of the egos that prevents a smooth relationship. More often than not the loser is the subordinate. It is good remember the law of return in behavioral situations that emphasizes that the giver gets back more than the receiver.

EXECUTIVE AS A BOSS

One of the basic functions of any executive is to get his/her subordinates to work together toward group goals. As a boss you should never lose sight of this objective and do everything in your power to ensure that everyone of your subordinates performs effectively what he/she is assigned to do. Their success is your success; their failure is your failure. Following are the desirable guidelines for the role of a good boss.

Be Fair to All

"Am I being fair to all of my subordinates?" is a question that you must ask yourself in dealing with more than one subordinates. No characteristic is more important than establishing a reputation for fairness for your long term success in people management. Fairness indicates your ability to deal with people as human beings and shows your respect for their individual rights and responsibilities.

Do not Show Favoritism

As a boss you should avoid showing open favoritism among the subordinates. Favoritism is an ethical and moral violation if not legal. Though it may not hurt you immediately, or in one instance, but it will in the long run when you develop a tendency to show favoritism. It is impossible to build a powerful team for your group goals if the team members do not believe that you are a fair-minded person.

Handling Complaints

Complaints are expressions of discontent from subordinates. The nature of the complaints can range from monetary benefits to sexual harassment in the work place. As a boss you should handle each complaint on its own merit. The first and foremost thing to do is to follow established guidelines to hear complaints in your organization. It is needed not only for legal purposes but also it gives an opportunity for proper documentation. Some complaints are likely to be resolved in the process without the need to reach the boss.

It is essential that you get a complete and undistorted picture of the complaint so that you can attend to it in an unbiased manner. Remember that you are acting as a judge in a courtroom and your decision is as significant as the judge's. Again, being fair-minded is what needed for an impartial resolution of the complaint.

Ability to Listen

As a boss it is essential than an executive develops the habit of attentive listening. Listening with concentration helps absorb most of what is heard and commits to memory. Whereas disinterested listening conveys to the speaker that you have no regard for his/her feelings. Attentive listening is a prerequisite for handling verbal complaints effectively.

Don't make the mistake of trying to fake listening. You don't fool anyone but yourself. Your face is the mirror of your mind; the speaker sees it and you don't.

If You Have to Fire or Lay off

When you are a boss it is inevitable that you will be faced with a situation to fire or lay-off one or more of your employees or subordinates sometime or other. It is a traumatic experience which many an executive is very uncomfortable to deal with.

You should learn to take an objective look at the process in a non-emotional manner and handle the dismissal in a civic manner, wishing the fired or laid-off employee good luck elsewhere. Remember that he/she is as much a human being as you are, and treating him/her with dignity and respect will make you feel good later, if not at the time of confrontation.

Create Opportunities for Growth

As a boss, your primary interest, of course, is to get the best performance from your subordinates. Yet, in that process you should try to create and share opportunities for career growth within the department or organization as a whole. Such a broad-minded policy of a boss has the potential to infuse more enthusiasm and a spirit of teamwork among the subordinates. It is human nature to look for change and growth, and he/she is a wise executive who tries to go along human nature.

Reward for Good Performance

No boss in a private or public organization, small or large, can afford to overlook the principle of rewarding superior performance, if he/she is interested in the long-span welfare of the organization. Since no two human beings are the same, there is a wide range of difference in their approach to work among the subordinates or employees of any organization. some work with more enthusiasm and produce more than others in the same job requirement. Some go beyond the call of duty and serve as motivator for others as well. These individuals approach their work as if it is a source of joy, and it is for them. You should try to spot out these people and reward them in a suitable manner as a gesture of appreciation on your part. The reward can be a pat on the back, certificate of meritorious service, salary rise, or promotion to new job responsibilities.

EXECUTIVE TIME MANAGEMENT

Time Versus Activity

Executive excellence is a myth if the executive does not have a complete mastery over his/her time. Time, unlike other commodities, comes one day at a time for everyone from the lowest subordinate to the highest boss. Of course, your time is more valuable to you than to others. Since you can not add to or subtract from your available time, it is primarily a question of management and utilization of time for the activities that you desire to carry out. Time and activity go hand in glove such as thirty minutes of walking, studying, resting, etc. You must realize that it is the activity that you are engaged in that results in the desired effect and not time per se.

Time and Money

For all practical purposes time is on a par with money. Both can be invested, expended, and wasted. Unlike money, time is available to you just one day at a time as the gift of life, and it is up to you to utilize it for your maximum benefit. While a person can choose to accumulate a substantial amount of money, no one can accumulate time. It can only be used more efficiently.

Time spent on activities that enhance your performance as an executive is a good investment. Time spent in normal sleeping, eating, getting ready to go to office and in other chores of daily routines can be considered as a necessary expenditure. Time spent in oversleeping, and in non-productive activities which are neither planned towards your goals nor for the maintenance of your bodily and mental well-being is a shear waste of your precious life energy. Time is obviously more valuable than money; lost money can be recovered, but not lost time.

Time Budget

Budgeting your time is the key in time management. Since the available time everyday is a limited quantity, it is of paramount importance that you budget out your time to the various activities which you have planned for the day. Budgeting prevents the waste of your precious time and lets you invest it on task-oriented and goal-achieving activities.

Time Drain and Lack of Self-discipline

While budgeting lets you plan to apportion your available time for routine and planned activities, it does not guarantee their completion as planned all the time. Minor and major interruptions varying from phone-calls to prolonged meetings can easily derail your budget of good intentions. Often it is the lack of self-discipline on the part of the individual who allows himself/herself deviate far from the time budget. It is for you to recognize the time-draining activities that interrupt your time budget and put yourself on the time track.

Time for Planning and Review

Effective time management rests on the small amount of time spent on planning the time budget and reviewing the efficiency of the budget execution. On the face of it, this principle may not appear that important. Five minutes of planning in the morning before starting the day and five minutes of review before going to bed is probably your most productive activity keeping you oriented towards achieving success in your goals.

Time Pressure and Stress

Time pressure can induce psychosomatic responses. When the time and activities are not properly matched, that is, trying to accomplish too many things in too short a time, so-called time-pressure occurs and the unaccomplished activities induce frustration. Frustration is a common occurrence with executives trying to catch up with unfinished routine chores, progress reports, meetings, etc. Regardless of its source, frustration is an uncomfortable, unpleasant, and disturbing experience. It acts on the mind producing discomfort and a state of tension, commonly referred to as stress.

Minor frustrations are normal human reactions and are not harmful to the well-being of a person. However, persons with low frustration tolerance are easily affected by stress and can develop stress-related ailments such as migraine headaches, peptic ulcer, high blood pressure, asthma, and skin rashes to mention a few.

Personal Time Analysis

Personal time analysis is the key for mastery and effective utilization of your time. Keep a record of time consumed for most of your activities, professional and personal, and also keep track of time spent on routine non-productive chores. Study carefully this record maintained for a week. You will be surprised to spot the many activities which you could have done in less time had you been more conscious of the time spent for them. This finding will serve as a time management guide for the following week and will save you the time unduly consumed in trivialities, both professional and personal.

"Workaholic" Time

Many an executive falls into the trap of workaholism by not being able to get things done during the normal working hours. They tend to extend their working hours after everyone has gone home or take the work home or work during weekends and holidays. There is no cure for the workaholic, unless he/she learns the technique of Personal Time Analysis and tries to implement time management, balancing his/her professional and personal lives.

Behavior psychologists consider workaholism as a learned escapism on the part of the executive who tries to avoid a stressful realism in another part of his/her life, complaining that there is no time. Of course, an executive may have need often to work longer and harder, but that should not lead him/her to workaholism when he/she becomes master of his/her time.

CHAPTER 5

S-SKILLS
(SYNERGISTIC SKILLS)

"One will achieve all that he desires, if he becomes resolute and determined".

Thiruvalluvar,
Thirukural (verse 666)

TOPICS

1. What are Synergistic Skills?
2. Vision and Visualization
3. Creative Innovation
4. Preventive Planning
5. Appointing Right Person for the Right Job
6. Team Building
7. Dealing with Fellow Executives
8. Recognizing Opportunities
9. Zeroing-in (Ability to Focus)
10. Crisis Management
11. Leadership

WHAT ARE S-SKILLS?

Synergism refers to the occurrence of a manifest effect which is much greater than the sum of all effects produced by individual contributing factors. In biology it refers to the action of two or more substances, organs, or organisms to achieve an effect of which each is individually incapable. In theology it means the doctrine that regeneration is effected by a combination of human will and divine goals.

In the business and professional world success is not an automatic outcome for the executives, managers, and professionals just because he/she possesses all the skills we mentioned in earlier chapters such as the R-Skills and the M/A-Skills. Those skills, nevertheless, are needed for effective functioning and subtle efficiency in the job performance. But something else is needed for excellence in performance. And that is a set of additional skills and characteristics—not possessed by every executive. They are not taught in management schools nor can be transmitted by word of mouth. I prefer to call them "synergistic skills" (S-Skills) because these skills when applied together with the previously mentioned "R" and "M/A" skills have been found to produce synergistic effect in the overall performance of executives.

There is no hard and fast method of teaching "S" skills. It is for the individual to develop them subjectively by being aware of them and their due place in his/her functioning as an executive, manager, or professional. Awareness is the first step in the conscious development of any desired personal characteristics and qualities. If you analyze the job performance of the so-called "super-executives" whom you personally know and respect, you will find them possessing one or more of these "S" skills presented below. It is up to you to learn more about the "S" skills and integrate them into your job performance. When you put them to practice, it is inevitable that synergistic results will follow. All executive entrepreneurs distinguish themselves only through these synergistic skills, or they would have been doomed to a life of mediocrity like others who work for them.

Following are the synergistic skills:
1. Vision and visualization
2. Creative innovation
3. Preventive planning

4. Appointing right person for the right job
5. Team building
6. Dealing with fellow executives
7. Recognizing opportunities
8. Zeroing-in (Ability to focus)
9. Crisis management
10. Leadership.

VISION AND VISUALIZATION

Vision

Vision implies foresight and anticipation. For the executive it means an ability to look at the horizon and develop a far reaching plan for the growth and welfare of the organization compatible to the society's present and future needs and the mission of the organization. It is this vision that has distinguished many a great entrepreneur. Even in humble and restrained business environments, it is the executive with a vision who makes the difference rather than the one who does not have any such vision but who just carries on with routine chores only.

Foresight can be intuitive or developed through the projection of past experiences. Foresight on the part of the executive in matters of administration, planning, and management can prevent critical even catastrophic situations in the life of the organization.

Meditation or contemplation is the right tool for developing vision in any field of activity. By pondering over and over again on a matter pertaining to your executive jurisdiction that requires your direct input, you can develop a vision in that area. It is the repeated contemplation that slowly crystallizes into a vision that becomes a part of your thinking, though for some it may appear intuitive.

Visualization

Visualization is a powerful technique widely used in modern psychology, sports, and even in medicine to develop skills at achieving goals. Visualization implies the formation of a mental image or a "picture" of whatever that is desired. Meditation and visualization are the two sides of the same coin, commonly referred to as subjective realization. Because of the subjective nature of the technique, the individual has to learn to visualize methodically and systematically.

Visualization as a technique is not the same as imagination though the latter also is involved in forming mental pictures. There is a subtle difference. Visualization is the process of creating visual images not present to the eye. It is an imagined scene with all its concreteness to become a part of your memory which is intended for repeated recall, whereas a casually imagined scene has no recall significance and thus lost to the memory. Visualization holds the key to unlock the higher reaches of one's own creative potentials.

When you create a vivid mental picture, your body actually responds to the visualization as if it were a real experience. Dr. Maxwell Maltz, in his book, Psycho-cybernetics, mentions that your nervous system can not tell the difference between an imagined experience and a real experience. In either case, it acts automatically to the information you provide from your forebrain. Your nervous system reacts appropriately to what you visualize, thus establishing a psychological response to the visualized imagery.

Dr. Kenneth R. Pelletier, in his book, Mind as Healer Mind as Slayer, mentions that the induced visualization can be employed to stimulate the creative imagination, and when used while in a state of passive concentration, it is a very powerful tool to mobilize the resources of both the body and mind.

The Technique

1. Sit in the meditative position with your eyes closed and slowly bring yourself to the alpha state of relaxation.
2. Visualize a concept, dream, or vision for your organization and for your yourself. Make it as vivid as possible adding details pretty much the same manner an artist creates a scene on canvas. Hold the visualized image in your mind for about 15 minutes and live through it again and again during this session.
3. Next day, again, go over the same process recalling to your mind from memory the previously visualized imagery. Dwell on it for about 15 minutes.
4. Make the session of visualization a routine everyday, preferably at the same time and place. Gradually, whatever you had visualized begins to crystallize as a part of your living experience, and your thoughts and actions will begin to get oriented

towards this new experience. It will become a permanent part of your memory, and it will be available for recall anytime anywhere by you. Of course, the success is dependent on your self-disciplined approach to the sessions of visualization.

CREATIVE INNOVATION

Innovation, undoubtedly, is one of the major elements of success in the history of many successful organizations and executives. To perceive and introduce something new in any or many operational areas such as product design, manufacture, service, advertising, marketing, etc., has become almost a need for organizational survival in today's highly competitive national and international milieu. No company or corporation can afford to stay in business for long without bringing in innovation of some kind from time to time.

That being the case, it is for the executive to develop in himself/herself the skill of creative innovation. It may appear on the face that the talent for creativity is not for all. But, this is not the case. Modern psychologists and anthropologists concur that creativity is an inherited potential in human organisms and thus every human being has it in one form or another. It is immediately evident in some and remains dormant in others till an appropriate environment develops. By being aware of this fact, you as an executive can certainly examine the ways and means of introducing creative innovation in your operational jurisdiction. With an eye on innovation, you should encourage creativity in others working with you.

Creative innovation need not necessarily be spectacular. Even small improvements are creative in nature, and as such, constant small improvements in all spheres of organizational operations will contribute towards excellence.

PREVENTIVE PLANNING

Preventive planning should not be confused with functional or growth planning. Functional planning serves the day to day operational aspects of the organization for a smooth functioning as a system in its various fronts. Growth planning, as the name indicates, provides for an orderly growth and expansion of the organization to integrate its long-term goals.

Preventive planning, on the other hand, aims at steps that must be taken to locate possible trouble spots both in the functional as well as the growth planning and provide for their resolution. In addition it should anticipate fluctuations in the socio-economic, even political, milieu in the organizational interaction and provide for possible negative changes that may be detrimental for the welfare of the organization.

Of course, it is impossible to "crystal gaze" and foresee all that is there in store for the future. But as a principle, preventive planning can make the winning or losing difference between success and failure of an organization. In fact, preventive planning is of paramount importance in operations which depend on something else for their functioning such as in manufacture and production.

Apart from professional and career related situations, in personal life also preventive planning plays a major role, particularly in personal financial management and stress management. The executive with a flair for preventive planning, personal and organizational, will not be taken by surprise by catastrophic or failure threatening situations.

Preventive planning as a skill lies in your ability when you pay attention to the cause and effect relation in every situation and see short-range difficulties in the light of long-range goals.

APPOINTING RIGHT PERSON FOR THE RIGHT JOB

Ability to select and appoint a right person for the right job is more than a skill. There is more to appointing a person than just the consideration of academic qualifications and job skill. It involves certain principles which the executive should be aware of. Of all the executive skills, this is probably the single most sensitive issue in any organization, public or private, small or large, and also in government.

Relatives

Appointment of relatives, however well qualified, to key positions in your jurisdiction must be avoided. Sooner or later interpersonal problems are likely to develop because of the difficulty in exercising executive authority on them. Tolerance towards relatives in the office may send wrong message to other employees who will develop resentment. It is a wise executive who keeps himself/herself clear of relatives in his/her career and professional life.

Skill Plus Compatibility

Examine the credentials and look for a person who has not only the necessary knowledge and skill but who also is compatible to your personality and to your organizational objectives and goals. Examine the psychological traits of the person to find out more about his/her personality profile. Will he/she be reliable? Will he/she be loyal? Will he/she be able to get things done? Since every human being has his/her own faults and shortcomings, you should not expect a perfect match for the job or position. Settle on a person who has created an overall plus feeling in you.

Responsibility Plus Power

Once you have made up your mind from all considerations, assign the responsibility to the person and give him/her the necessary authority to carry out the job function. You may have the person report to you periodically but you should not interfere into his/her operational jurisdiction.

Watch out for Attitude Change

Many a person has been known to show marked changes in their attitudes negatively and detrimental to the employer and the organization after they had been appointed. This change takes place due to the very nature of the job function and the power associated with the position, however well you might have screened them before hiring. It is essential that you keep track of the job performance and any negative attitudes of the appointee so that you can take appropriate action before the person becomes a liability to you.

TEAM BUILDING

The strength of the executive lies in his/her team who directly report to him/her. It is not much different from the strength of a general related to his ability to have his officers under his command knit into a harmonious unit who will carry out his orders so that he can make the strategic moves and planning. The group compatibility within the team and a sense of loyalty towards the executive and the organization are factors that can not be induced or created by any executive order or memo.

Building a compatible team requires an intuitive understanding of human behavior on your part. For the team members to accept your leadership and lend their full support to you, you must be able to command their confidence in you and in their faith that they can rely on you for their own career and professional advancement. You should be able to anticipate their expectation and demonstrate your support for them at the right places at right moments so that they stand to gain promotion, rise in salary, division control, etc., which will enhance their self-esteem.

Of course, you can not always go to their rescue and give them something every time; they also know it. What counts is the creation in their minds the feeling that you will not let them down when they rightfully deserve a reward of some kind, and that you will fight from their side with the higher-ups when they are on the right.

Favoritism

The key to getting full support from the team members lies in your playing fair with all of them without any favorites. It is a psychological truth that no human being can tolerate preferential treatment of another who is equally placed. Favoritism breeds silent ill-will and subtly destroys the very fabric of team-work when the executive leader is guilty of it.

DEALING WITH FELLOW EXECUTIVES

On a casual consideration, the ability to deal with fellow executives may not appear difficult, but every executive in his/her heart of hearts knows the possible eruption of anger and frustrations in the relationship. Open rivalry and enmity among executives at the same rank as well as in the hierarchy is not uncommon in big organizations. In his book, "Developing Your Executive Skills", Auren Uris mentions that lateral contacts tend to be a big blind spot in the job life of many executives. It mainly arises from two conflicting basic pressures on the executive that work in opposite directions: personal competition and mutual interests.

Personal Competition

It is a hard reality of executive life that everyone at the same rank is a competitor for the boss's position, or advancement due to the pyramid structure of the hierarchial command in almost all organizations of corporate nature. In the typical situation there is either an open or covert struggle for power, and for status. It is not surprising, then, for competitors to be unfriendly to each other.

Mutual Interest

You and your fellow executives are very frequently in the same boat, whether you like it or not. You may have the same kind of problems with the same superior, and it will be to your common interest to forge a friendly relation with your fellow executives to safeguard your territory, if not for anything else. Again, you and your peers must strive and achieve within the organizational and policy framework of the same company. Your needs, hopes, and aspirations may frequently by identical.

Being torn between these two opposing forces of personal competition and mutual interests, very few executives are wise enough to handle the conflict without being unduly stressed. Competition between equals is not only natural, but can also be productive. But situations and personalities, more often than not, tend to heighten and manifest antagonism, which, of course, is not desirable from a professional point of view though one may feel justified from a personal point of view. What is desirable is a common sense approach of opening the door of communication and cooperation.

Positive Steps

1. **Communication.** Setting up communications exchange sessions, and informal discussions on matters of mutual interest will lessen the tension between you and your fellow executive. Be open and willing to share information of common interest which may be more helpful to him/her than to you.

2. **Cooperation.** Remember that cooperation is a give-and-take proposition. Of course you will always find executives who are ready to take but not to give, but when you act within the dictates of your conscience you will soon begin to get cooperation from others. It is a law of return in human behavior.

3. **Eliminate friction.** Trying to know the fellow executive and understand his/her way of doing things will pave the way for better relationships. Understand the pressure under which he/she operates. They are probably like yours, personal problems on one hand and deadlines on the other. Try to understand his/her behavioral response pattern and personality. This will help in dealing with that person in tight situations which might otherwise precipitate a crisis. Don't underestimate the importance of contacts with fellow executives outside working hours. View every company function, lunch, dinner and conference as an opportunity for better relations.

4. **Build for friendship.** For your part, start with the strong foundations of good intentions and good will. Improving relations with your fellow executives should be a long-term objective. It is inevitable that you may have to face the likelihood of disagreements which can be very strong. Yet, there is no better method to solving this than a face-to-face discussion, keeping the emotions at bay.

"Mending the fence", as the saying goes, is undoubtedly a positive step in building better future relations for mutual interests. Offer him/her help whenever you can; if it is done sincerely the return in goodwill is practically certain.

RECOGNIZING OPPORTUNITIES

To be able to recognize opportunities for organizational and/or personal growth and advancement is a skill that can not be developed like other skills such as painting, hunting, etc. Opportunities are not perceived by all persons at the same time however obvious they may look to those who can recognize them. Ability to recognize them is considered partly intuitive and partly analytic. A wider and deeper knowledge in the specific subject area makes the difference from an analytical point of view. The executive who has the combination of an intuitive and analytical frame of mind undoubtedly holds the edge over others who are routine-task oriented. Ability to recognize opportunities becomes a synergistic characteristic for the executive who possesses reinforcer and management skills as we had outlined in earlier chapters to a reasonable degree.

Career advancement for you as an executive is dependent on this ability to recognize opportunities within your organization and without as well. When your fellow executives are reluctant to initiate or continue a difficult assignment, the one who can willingly undertake it sees it as an opportunity for personal advancement, which may not be immediately evident for others. The efforts to gain experience in new or different areas of professional operation is a worthy investment for future advancement.

Outside of the organization, the economic and political environment is constantly undergoing changes and technological innovations are reshaping the world we live in. There is no dearth for opportunities for one who can keep an open eye and is willing to take a plunge.

ZEROING-IN (ABILITY TO FOCUS AND ACT)

Another ability of synergistic nature for the executive is to be able to zero-in on whatever project he/she has undertaken. In fact, recognizing an opportunity by itself has no value unless it is followed by concerted effort to go after the goals set to utilize the opportunity. Zeroing-in refers to the planning and action part needed to make the opportunity pay off.

Thiruvalluvar, the 3rd century B.C. philosopher and author of Thirukural, enumerates six steps needed for zeroing-in. Their validity has endured the centuries and they are more valid today than ever before. The sequence of steps are:

1. Goal-oriented action plan
2. Resources collection
3. Selection of experts
4. Choice of time for action
5. Choice of location
6. Action.

Once an opportunity is recognized, the first and foremost thing to do is to formulate an action plan with attainable goals in a meaningful time frame. The next step is to collect resources and materials appropriate to the action plan. This also implies being prepared with financial backing necessary for the venture. Choosing the right experts for action and/or advice is the third step. Even when the executive himself/herself is an expert in the subject area of the venture undertaken, he/she will be a wise person to solicit suggestions and advice before embarking on the action plan.

The executive must now pay special attention to the choice of right time for action. Time as a critical element in the action plan can not be overstated. There is no substitute for timely action. Timely action can save lives, win wars, and in the corporate and business world can spell the difference between success and failure of their operations.

Another element of equal importance is the choice of location for the proposed activity. It must be compatible to the activity. There is no dearth for examples of ventures that failed due to wrong location in spite of all the available resources and excellent planning.

Finally, attention must be paid to the action itself. This is the execution part of the action plan and it requires a concerted effort on the part of all concerned. If the venture or assignment is an one-man operation, the executive should go after the completion of the goal-oriented activities step by step exactly the same way as outlined.

CRISIS MANAGEMENT

Crisis is an unanticipated occurrence or event in life of a person for which he/she is not prepared. Crisis can come in many different forms—sudden death of a beloved person, divorce, job lay-off, financial losses, accidents, catastrophic illness or sickness of oneself or loved ones, etc. Two factors contribute to the intensity of the crisis— one is the unexpected nature and the other the unpreparedness to deal with the event.

A crisis is extremely stressful for the simple reason that the person undergoes an utter feeling of helplessness. Nothing precipitates emotional stress more than being in a state of helplessness, real or imagined. The result is that the person becomes overly emotional, displaying the basic raw emotions of anger, fear, or grief, even joy, depending on the nature of the event causing the crisis. The emotional response of individuals, of course, varies—some overly react, whereas some are able to handle the crisis with restraint, depending on their mental make-up or what is generally called as their personality.

Crisis in the life of organizations is not much different from that in the life of individuals in the two principal factors of occurrence, namely, the unexpectedness and unpreparedness. It may not be with the same catastrophic suddenness as in the life of an individual, but slowly it begins to precipitate when the conditions conducive for crisis are present and undermines the financial and/or executive stability of the organization.

Ability to deal with crisis in personal life is an index of the emotional maturity of the person. It is a synergistic skill for the executive as far as the organization is concerned. The executive who is capable of managing crisis in personal life can be expected to deal with organizational crisis in a more rational manner than one who is unduly stressed in personal crisis situations.

Is crisis preventable? Many a time, yes—say behavior psychologists. Anticipation of a potential crisis provoking event and being prepared mentally and action-wise to face it and deal with it are the best means of prevention. The state of being prepared eliminates the feeling of helplessness in the face of the impending crisis, thereby reducing its traumatic intensity.

Behind every crisis lies an opportunity for its prevention in the future, provided we take time to analyze the cause and effect of the crisis and adopt an action plan designed to deal with it preventively.

LEADERSHIP

What is Leadership?

In its simplest form, leadership is the skill or ability to guide by showing the way or to command and direct. It also implies the ability to induce in others a willingness to accept and to follow—often referred to as the ability to motivate others.

Contrary to what most people believe, leadership is not something that a person is blessed with at birth. But the characteristics that contribute to leadership are acquired. It can therefore be developed and improved. Leadership for the executive can not easily be separated out of his/her overall executive ability. Getting your subordinates to work together toward group goals, for example, is both a leadership as well as executive function.

Leadership is not an all-or-nothing skill. It is not that either you have it or don't have it. Leadership is more appropriately considered in relation to the conditions under which you operate, rather than to some abstract, arbitrary rules of do's and don'ts.

Three Types of Leadership

To get the most from a group of individuals working together towards common goals is best accomplished when one person is charged with the responsibility of achieving the goals. For all practical purposes this person is considered as the leader of the group and it is for him/her to deal with the different personalities of the group such that each person contributes optimally. Three different approaches in leadership have generally been known to be most effective in dealing with most people. Briefly on principle they are:

Autocratic leadership. The leader assumes full responsibility for all action. He/she issues orders and seeks obedience from the group in following his/her orders. All policies are determined by the leader, and all decision-making are also done by him/her.

Democratic leadership. The leader draws ideas and suggestions from the group by discussion and consultation. Group members are encouraged to take part in setting policies. The player plays the role of a moderator.

Supportive leadership. In this approach the leader plays mostly the role of a supporter attending to the needs of the group members. He/she is on hand mainly to provide materials and information, with a minimum of control.

As an executive you should consider that these three basic methods of leadership are but three tools available to you for appropriate application with your group. These three approaches are not mutually exclusive. It is for you to use your judgment diligently in getting work done through one or more of these approaches suiting the person and the situation. Some people respond better to autocratic leadership, some to democratic, and yet others to supportive type of leadership.

What Makes an Effective Leader?

This is one of the most often asked questions regarding leadership. There is no one answer to this question. A person who can motivate others to follow his lead, of course, should have certain distinct characteristics which are respected by his followers. Leadership is both situational and temporal. But, anyone who thinks that he is born to lead assumes basically dictatorial characteristics, and no dictator has lasted long.

It is essential that you don't fall into the trap of assuming autocratic or democratic leadership all the time with all the members of your group. It is the surest way of building resentment from your subordinates and you will not get their optimum performance. It is here your skill at leadership becomes distinctly synergistic when you distinguish the personality types in your group and recognize the most effective leadership approach to which the person is most responsive.

CHAPTER 6

SITUATIONAL TACTICS AND TIPS

"(When you have enemies) do not openly show your enmity; the wise will hold the anger inside of them, waiting for the right opportunity to strike."

Thiruvalluvar,
Thirukural, (verse 487)

TOPICS

1. Tactics and Their Proper Use
2. Praises and Promises
3. Smile and Frown
4. Respect Other People's Egos
5. Never Lose Your Temper
6. Listen to Grapevine but Don't Gossip
7. Ally Yourself with the Power People
8. Tell the Boss What He/She Wants to Hear
9. Loyalty—Take It with a Pinch of Salt
10. Build a Network of Business Friends
11. Keep Romance out of Office
12. Build Yourself a Business Image
13. Build Yourself a Power Base
14. Be Prepared for Changes and Challenges

15. Handle Your Enemies with Care
16. Learn Diplomacy—the Master Art of Office Politics
17. Give Recognition Where Due
18. Keep Your Door Open for Suggestions and Criticisms
19. Be Assertive but Be on the Right
20. Honesty Is the Best Policy
21. Keep Off the Bottle
22. Put It in Writing
23. Refer to a Committee
24. Act, Don't React
25. Silence—Maintain Your Confidences
26. Consult with Experts when You Don't Know
27. Give Respect Get Respect
28. Don't Brag—Let Your Actions Speak
29. Don't Burn Your Bridges Behind You
30. Socialize without Losing Your Personality
31. Focus on a Specific Goal

TACTICS AND THEIR PROPER USE

Tactics! Most people don't like to discuss it but nevertheless use it! Tactics imply manipulating people and it is not acceptable in any cultured society to appear as if one is manipulating others. Yet, there is need for executives, managers, and administrators to manipulate people and structure situations to get things done, and also to get ahead in a competitive environment. Goal achievement, personal or organizational, for an executive depends on a plan of action or strategy which he/she conceives. To carry out the strategies, though, he/she needs proper tactics. Sound strategies can fail if not executed through proper tactics.

There is no way of avoiding or being ignorant of tactics for an executive, if he/she wants to be effective in his/her job performance. A tactic, in effect, is a tool or an item of knowledge for the executive, and there is nothing mystical about knowledge. Any tactic by itself is neither good nor bad. Ethical questions are concerned only on how it is used. Therefore, the concern for the executive is to decide on applying appropriate tactics most suited for the situation. It is akin to choosing the right tool for the right job.

In his book "The Corporate Prince", Qass Aquarius states that the tactics one selects should depend upon his own personality, the personalities of the other people involved in the action, the importance of the situation, the urgency of the matter, the relationships of the parties involved and their relative powers, and other unclassifiable random factors that always exist in administrative situations.

In "Thirukural" Thiruvalluvar states that a tactic adopted by the executive in order to be effective should be viewed from the combined factors of time, place, the persons involved, the situation and the possible outcome. Just because a tactic was successful in one situation once before it should not be used indiscriminately in other situations without paying attention to the combination of the factors mentioned.

Tactics reflect the psychological maturity and the depth of understanding of human behavior on the part of the executive. So long as he/she is able to use tactics to safeguard the interests of himself/herself and those of others under his/her leadership and stay within legal bounds, no harm is done—though the adversaries may criticize the person as being cunning, scheming, calculating, and the like. Remember, your success is the same no matter by what name enemies call it.

PRAISES AND PROMISES

It is human nature to feel elated and be pleased when someone praises us for our actions and accomplishments however small they may appear to be. As an executive you should take full advantage of this simple principle and apply it diligently in your interactions with your boss, peers, and subordinates.

Praises and compliments must be genuine in the first place. They must be brief, casual, and never elaborated. A smile on your face and a direct look at the person have the potential to make him/her feel the genuineness and warmth of your compliments. Remember the simple rule—if you do not mean it, do not say it.

Promise is a different matter. Promise and hope are directly related. The one who receives a promise nurtures hopes of getting it. Disappointment and resentment are the natural outcome of unfulfilled promises which can affect the smooth interpersonal relations between the promisor and the promised. As a boss, occasionally you may find yourself in a tight spot where a promise may seem to be the only logical solution. For example: an efficient worker whom you like is asking for a rise in salary, or the situation where you spot an excellent candidate you are interviewing for a position under your supervision, but you didn't have immediate authority to grant the monetary remuneration and other benefits the candidate is seeking.

In such a situation, no matter how you feel, do not promise anything that you can not deliver. Promise is a promise—your reputation is at stake. It won't take long for others to know about the resentment and ill-will of those who were promised. Nothing is more damaging for an executive than being branded as one who can not or will not keep his/her promises.

SMILE AND FROWN

Everyone likes a smiling face. "Smile and the world smiles with you"—says an old adage. In office situations you can use smile as an act of approval. Besides, a smile creates a congenial environment for all kinds of interpersonal relations. It particularly puts a subordinate in a comfortable position to air his/her opinion or complaints to the boss, which otherwise would have been difficult. You can also use smile as a mask to cover your personal feelings which you don't want to reveal in some circumstances.

On the same token, you can use frown as an expression of your dissatisfaction and displeasure. But you must be very careful in frowning, confining it only to situations which may need a mild reprimand from you and no more. Frown, like smile, is a potential image-maker and frequent display of them can make you being viewed as an unfriendly and difficult personality.

RESPECT OTHER PEOPLE'S EGOS

Remember the psychological truth that the center stage of everyone's life is his/her ego to which everything else is tied for that person. When you deal with superiors you will realize that it is their egos that is subtly visible in the forefront of their achievements. Similarly when you deal with people under you, you must respect the fact that their egos are bound with their desire for success and acceptance as much as yours is. It is not any different in the case of your peers either.

What is important is that you should learn to be sensitive to the ego aspect of people with whom you are dealing with at any given time—that means not to hurt or disregard their feelings. Effective interpersonal relations is a myth for the executive who can not comprehend the ego aspect of people working with and for him.

NEVER LOSE YOUR TEMPER

If there is anything that is going to win friends in the long run in personal and professional life, it is your ability to control the emotional part of your inner self. It is one thing to become emotional and it is another to try to manage the emotions. To become emotional is easy and natural; to control emotions is difficult and needs self-control and discipline.

As an executive you will find yourself in many situations which can provoke your emotions, particularly anger. You may become angry with the boss for giving you an assignment with a tight deadline when you have other plans; you may be angry with him/her for denying you the promotion and salary rise you deserve; you may be angry with your peers for interfering in your jurisdiction; you may be angry with your sub-ordinate for not carrying out your instructions

Remember, in the interest of long-term career success, do not lose your temper under any circumstances. Each anger provoking situation should be handled on its own merit with your appropriate response. It is your response the other person is going to see and not what went on in your mind. Your response should be rational and intellectual and never emotional. Losing temper destroys the good will of others and breeds resentment and enmity. Effective executive performance requires an even temper in interpersonal relations at all levels.

LISTEN TO THE GRAPEVINE BUT DON'T GOSSIP

The grapevine is an integral part of internal group communication in any organization which thrives on human nature to gossip. Gossip it may be, but there also may be an element of truth behind the matter. You may hear the grapevine at corridors, elevators, water coolers, rest rooms and lunchrooms.

As an executive you should not contribute to grapevine. Never gossip with your fellow employees within office premises. You must maintain your image of dignity. However, that should not prevent you from keeping your ears open to listen to what is being talked about around you. While you should discount the sensational aspect of the floating news, be sure not to let go the element of truth behind them. Often you can learn about many important top level decisions and happenings of the organization ahead of time through the grapevine. That piece of information might be of some importance to you to make a tactical move in your bid for moving up or outwit your adversary.

ALLY YOURSELF WITH THE POWER PEOPLE

If your goal is to move up in the hierarchy in your organization, nothing is more important than your alinement with the people who wield real power in the organization. This does not mean to say that you alienate others. The point is to recognize the fact that the people in power want to promote to top positions those whom they can trust and with whom they are comfortable to share the line of command. Your alinement is a powerful indicator and a conveyor of message about your support and willingness to go along with them.

Your indication of alinement is all the more important in organizations where struggle for power is in the open at the top level. On the same token, you must realize that support and loyalty to a losing person can mean the loss of your own job if that person is thrown off.

The game of alinement should be played in a very subtle manner, avoiding any direct confrontation with those in power.

TELL THE BOSS WHAT HE/SHE WANTS TO HEAR

You don't have to go out of the way to please your boss, and it is not that the boss must be pleased every time. Tell the boss what he/she wants to hear in matters of general nature concerning the department or division without lying. It is important that you never overstep the line of honesty no matter whether the boss is pleased or not. Pleasing the boss without telling lies on matters he/she wants to hear is a pleasantry that can build goodwill with the boss.

A good boss will gauge a worker or subordinate by the performance and not just by words. Pleasantry is not a substitute for good job performance.

LOYALTY—TAKE IT WITH A PINCH OF SALT

Loyalty undoubtedly is a noble virtue to follow—in the right environment. However, in a corporate milieu of a free enterprise society things can change so fast that loyalty can find itself in trouble. Also, when you have aims to move up the hierarchy of the corporate ladder you should be careful in placing your loyalty in the right basket.

Of course, you should be thankful to a boss who gave you something as a rise or a promotion; but that should not lock yourself into an abiding loyalty to that person, particularly when he/she is in a losing situation with his/her higher-ups. Treat your loyalty with a pinch of salt. When a corporation has no hesitation to throw you off your job for reasons not related to your job performance, your loyalty has little meaning to your employer. Like in a game of musical chair, be ever alert to safeguarding your position for survival first, success later.

BUILD A NETWORK OF BUSINESS FRIENDS

No matter what career or profession you are pursuing, the importance of having good business friends can not be overemphasized. Building a network of friends helps in the long run to enrich your career as well as personal life. Compatibility of personalities is an important element in developing any friendship. You should therefore be selective in the choice of friends.

Friendship is strengthened by interactive experiences, such as spending time together in playing games like golf, tennis, etc. Nurturing the friendship with occasional gifts, dinners, and inquiring phone calls, and showing a readiness to help when needed tend to keep the friendship alive and well.

On the same token you must be aware that it is a waste of time and energy trying to befriend people who are not compatible to you. Keep your business relations to the barest minimum with these people and keep yourself away from them socially and otherwise.

Business friendships have the potential to pave the way for more business opportunities. Some of the business friends can also develop into good personal friends. However strong the friendship is, you should remember that it is fragile and brittle, and you should handle it with utmost care and respect. It is something that you can not take for granted.

A word of caution in maintaining a healthy friendship is in order. Never try to take advantage of your friendship for personal, selfish gains. That is the surest way to destroy the friendship.

KEEP ROMANCE OUT OF OFFICE

Today's work place in office provides equal opportunity for women to compete and move upwards in the corporate ladder. Though men and women are considered simply as co-workers in the eyes of man-made law, situations do arise where the biological law of male-female attraction asserts itself. When two co-workers of the opposite sex are attracted to each other, the question arises: what is the right way to handle the relationship.

The most sensible rule to follow is: keep romance out of office. Romance in the work place in the presence of co-workers and the boss has many pitfalls. Ethical questions will be raised along with questions on effectiveness of job performance when the romance becomes public. There are jealous people around who may spread gossip about the relationship and do character assassination on the sly.

If you are really in love with each other, get one of you transferred to another office or division, and get married soon without giving room for loose talks and gossip!

BUILD YOURSELF A BUSINESS IMAGE

Pay special attention to build a personal business or professional image. Merely dressing well is not enough. Your image should have a personality of its own. It is formed through the consistent principles and habits with which you carry out your business routines and dealing with people as observed by others. Coming to office in the morning, leaving it in the evening, going to meetings on time, intent listening when talked to, dressing well, smiling whenever you meet peers and subordinates in the hallway, never losing temper in business matters, exchanging a pleasant word or a polite good-morning with fellow workers no matter what rank they are in, are but a few items of image makers.

For Female Executives:

In addition to the above generalized principles of office behavior, you may like to pay more attention to dress. George Mazzi, author of "Moving up", mentions: "establish a personal style of dressing, expressing your business image through your clothes, while staying within the parameters of proper corporate attire. Small items, such as a favorite item of jewelry—or no jewelry at all ever—can become part of your mystique".

BUILD YOURSELF A POWER BASE

No matter what organization you work for you should plan on having a professional or career "territory" for yourself. This territory is created by virtue of your career specialty and its importance to the employer even if it is within a conventional division or department. This is your base which should play a vital supporting role to the smooth running of your organization. In other words, you must strive to have something on which your employer should depend on. You base should be such that at time of layoffs your employer can not afford to let you go.

Obviously to create such a territory for yourself you must have both knowledge and experience. In your early years of career, you should pay attention to attend seminars and evening classes in your specialty subjects to increase your knowledge; also, you should volunteer, whenever opportunity permits, to work on varied assignments to gain the valuable experience. Remember that the power bases of executives and professionals are built on the dual components of knowledge and experience—without which one's career will be shaky, creating job stress.

BE PREPARED FOR CHANGES AND CHALLENGES

Change is the law of nature and is the very basis of progress of any kind. As an executive, don't lock yourself into stagnant attitudes and don't try to maintain the status quo of your method of management with no room for new ideas. The society around us is changing fast, and accordingly old ideas and attitudes can become increasingly obsolete. New laws are constantly passed that can have a profound effect on the work place ethics and the manner in which business is done. Technological innovations keep ushering in new products and demands for new services to handle them.

According to George Mazzei, "the best executives are the ones who can recognize valid changes, decipher them from passing fads, and plan accordingly. The basic interactions in business don't change much, but the kinds of people acting out the games do. The enlightened executive looks to the past to review the need for change, to the present to implement ideas for change, and to the future to ensure movement through change".

HANDLE YOUR ENEMIES WITH CARE

Office politics is rife with jealousy and rivalry, often locked into cut-throat competition for promotion, prestige, and power, particularly at the executive level. But yet all are working for the same goals of the organization. Whether you like it or not you have to deal with fellow executives who have their eyes set for the same promotion as you are, and also others whom you might have rubbed at the wrong place one time or another.

The most important thing to remember is not to confront your enemies openly in committee meetings and other situations in presence of other people. It will be a vital mistake on your part to throw a verbal attack at your adversary even when you are on the right. Any emotional outburst is a sign of immaturity at any level in general and the executive level in particular. It will do more harm than good.

Confront your enemies with composure and dignity. You don't have to be impolite because you don't like them. In fact, being polite and dealing with them the same way as you do with others but without letting them know of your feelings is the right response. Never refuse to cooperate if you are thrown into a same team; nothing could damage your reputation as a leader more than non-cooperation. Besides, it could be used against you in the future. Learn to coexist but be alert to opportunities to get ahead.

LEARN DIPLOMACY—THE MASTER ART OF OFFICE POLITICS

No office is without politics. There is no point in saying, "Oh! There is a lot of politics in my office; I don't like politics." Such statements are indicative of the inability of the person to comprehend the subtle nature of human interactions in the office environment where predictable movements do not always occur. Politics is another name for human behavior and manipulations.

It is to your advantage to take interest in understanding how human interactions take place in speech, actions, and maneuvers around you in your own organization. It may or may not be fair from your point of view and value system. Don't be complaining and criticizing verbally with colleagues and others. Of course, be bold enough to express your opinion where it counts in the right place, at the right time and with the right people. Always remember the first law of human behavior that everyone acts or behaves at his/her self-interest. You feel hurt only when someone else's interest clashes with yours.

Behavioral response, keeping your interest safeguarded, with minimum clash with the interests of others is generally known as diplomacy. Being diplomatic implies that you anticipate the effect of the impact of your words and deeds with peers, subordinates, and bosses. It also implies that you keep yourself clear of turbulence in day to day dealings in the office and in getting benefits for yourself in salary and promotions and better assignments in the long run. How best you are going to translate this principle into actions for your career is up to you.

Remember that being diplomatic in office does not necessarily mean being bad, cunning or conniving. It is only a tool for your survival and success in a cut-throat competitive corporate environment. Use the tool with discretion. All successful executives have learnt the art of diplomacy in their own way.

Next time when you do complain, criticize or praise, do it diplomatically—without jeopardizing your self-interest!

GIVE RECOGNITION WHERE DUE

Career success and effective executive performance requires many stepping stones and one of them is giving due recognition, no matter what level or rank it belongs to. It may be your fellow executive, or your secretary, or the mail carrier of your organization.

The second law of psychology asserts that everyone likes to be recognized. Desire for recognition is basically an urge for acceptance. Acknowledge the support you received even it is a part of the person's responsibility such as that given by peers who work for the common goal. Make a mention of it to your boss at an appropriate situation. You don't have to be afraid of giving recognition to your fellow executive on the ground that he/she may gain a more favorable impression than yourself with the boss. Your act of recognizing others is a leadership characteristic which will not go unnoticed by those higher in rank. Also, you gain the friendship and goodwill of your peer when he/she comes to know of your good word on his/her behalf.

Giving recognition is indicative of a broad and mature mind. As a principle it can never hurt you. Only small-minded people are afraid of giving recognition where due.

KEEP YOUR DOOR OPEN FOR SUGGESTIONS AND CRITICISMS

All organizations where are more than one person on the payroll will have personnel problems in one form or another. It is a wise executive who keeps the door open for suggestions and criticisms from peers and subordinates. The open door policy serves two purposes. One is to encourage new ideas and suggestions for improvement conceived by other people in the organization. New ideas can come from any level. Never let go an idea expressed by any person unexamined because it was proposed by a person in a lower rank. Give due recognition, when an idea or suggestion is accepted.

The second purpose is to let people voice their complaints without fear and let their steam off if they have any genuine gripe. It is easy to rectify and set right genuine complaints in their early stages when they are paid attention. Unless you create the impression that you are an open-minded and fair person, no one will come to your unloading their gripes. Of course, how to handle the criticism is up to you. Every complaint has two sides and it is for you to investigate further and take the right action to mitigate the complaint.

BE ASSERTIVE BUT BE ON THE RIGHT

As an executive you will face many situations where you may have direct confrontation with fellow executives and others. Remember that since an open confrontation can be very unpleasant and potentially emotional it must be treated with care at the rational level. No matter what the issue is you should ascertain what is right and stay on that side.

You can and should not be too assertive if you are doubtful of an issue, or on the wrong side of it. To assert yourself when you are on the wrong, even if you are the boss, will have a negative impact on the morale of the employees. A better way to handle a confrontation is at the talking level. If you are on the right, you don't have to fear anything and you don't have to compromise. But when you find yourself on the wrong side, be sure to apologize and let the other person have the pleasure of being assertive. Quit the confrontation and adopt a conciliatory tone.

HONESTY IS THE BEST POLICY

There is no substitute for honesty. Though the executive may encounter many situations where his/her actions may seem to bend rules and regulations for selfish ends, there should be no question of violating the principle of honesty. Honesty is being truthful in words and deeds to the best of one's knowledge and belief. Staying within the realm of honesty eliminates mental conflicts and prevents possible legal, moral, and ethical violations.

It may appear too naive to tell someone the need to be honest, but when you consider the woes of many executives, managers, and professionals stemming from dishonesty, it is worthwhile to remind yourself about the need to adopt the policy of honesty as a guiding principle.

KEEP OFF THE BOTTLE

Chances are that you know at least one person who has become an alcoholic. Think of the traumatic experiences that person and his/

her family go through. Countless successful careers and happy families have been destroyed by the addiction to the bottle. Of course, nobody starts with an intention to become an alcoholic. Yet, many a so-called "social drinker" has gradually fallen victim to the powerful grips of addiction.

The message is loud and clear. Alcohol is a drug and like any other drug, it must be handled with caution, discretion, and medical supervision where appropriate. If you do not want to give up alcoholic beverages altogether and want to remain as a social drinker, then you must follow the five principles of "intelligent drinking" laid out by the American Medical Association:

1. **Set Reasonable Limits for Yourself**
   Do not exceed a pre-decided number of drinks on a given occasion, and stick to your decision. No more than two beers or two cocktails a day is a reasonable limit.

2. **Learn to Say NO**
   When you have reached the sensible limit you have set for yourself, politely but firmly refuse to exceed it, no matter who puts pressure on you.

3. **Drink Slowly**
   Do not gulp down a drink. Choose your drinks wisely for their flavor, not their "kick", and enjoy the taste of each sip.

4. **Dilute Your Drinks**
   If you prefer cocktails to beer, try to have long drinks. Instead of drinking your gin or whisky straight, drink it diluted with a mixer such as tonic, water, or soda water, in a tall glass.

5. **Do Not Drink on Your Own**
   Make it a point to confine your drinking only to social gatherings, and never drink alone. The urge to relax yourself at the end of a hard day with an alcoholic beverage can be as well satisfied with a cup of coffee or a soft drink over a television program or with a good book to read.

PUT IT IN WRITING

"Put it in writing" is a sound principle for the executive which serves two purposes. Since it is impossible to remember details of all events and details in the executive life, putting things in writing then and there and keeping the notes in an organized manner for immediate retrieval serves as a memory aid in the first place. Undoubtedly effective performance in any profession depends on a good memory and the memory aids in any form.

Putting it in writing serves another important purpose. It becomes the permanent and undisputed record of what happened in the past, and as such it becomes a powerful legal weapon. Its role is particularly significant in the interpersonal relations of your employees and also your own dealings with your bosses. For your own protection, before firing any of your subordinates, you would be better off documenting the series of violations by issuing memos and having them signed by the employee. On the same token, be sure to have the promises of your boss related to salary rises and promotions in writing. In the corporate world unwritten promises don't mean much.

REFER TO A COMMITTEE

On issues that may hurt you either way by virtue of your taking or not taking an individualistic decision, it will be wiser to refer the matter to a committee. Since a committee decision is impersonal, it eliminates any blame on the executive.

A word of caution: referring crucial issues to committees can also backfire. It can damage your reputation as an executive decision maker, when word goes around that you are too indecisive or rely on too many committees.

ACT, DON'T REACT

Learning to hold your composure under provoking circumstances is essential for you not only as an executive but also as a human being in day to day interactions with other people. Emotional blast-off at other people is the surest way to kill future relationships and breed a hidden sense of dislike for you. You may be able to get away with yelling and shouting at another person just because you are the boss once or twice, but the other person can not be expected to have any respect for you. He/she will nurture dislike and hatred which will find its expression against your interest in its own way sooner or later, particularly if you had hurt his/her self-respect.

No matter how much provoking the situation is, such as an obvious mistake committed by one of your subordinates, you should maintain evenness of temper and say or do things that are more rational rather than emotional. A well-thought out response in interpersonal relations is a sign of emotional maturity. It is the very foundation of superior executive performance.

SILENCE—MAINTAIN YOUR CONFIDENCES

It is natural that during the course of your tenure you will come across much confidential information related to personal or organizational events and dealings. It is of paramount importance that you maintain your silence and never discuss them with others. There may be times when your bosses may confide in you some secrets of their personal life—particularly during socializing time in parties or under the influence of alcohol. Keeping the information within yourself will win you more friends than you may be aware of. Building a reputation for yourself that you will never divulge secrets is a very desirable characteristic which is a hallmark of successful executives.

On the same token, it does not take long for people to know who lets out confidential information or treats lightly secrets in personal and corporate matters. No executive with such a bad reputation can expect to climb up the corporate ladder too far up.

CONSULT WITH EXPERTS WHEN YOU DON'T KNOW

Often executives tend to postpone decisions in important matters for lack of proper knowledge. No executive can know all about everything he/she is dealing with and the logical thing to do is to consult with one or more experts. Bringing in a consultant at the right time can mean a lot for the organization. With the new information and knowledge provided by the expert the executive will be in a better position to take decisions on issues he/she was hesitant before.

GIVE RESPECT GET RESPECT

It is a human need to feel respected, more so for the executive who is in a leadership position as far as subordinates are considered. There is nothing more demeaning for the executive than not being respected by people in his/her own division or department. It is not something to be automatically expected by virtue of being in a higher rank or position in a hierarchy.

Respect is a two-way street. No one who does not give respect can get respect. It is a fundamental law of human nature that people subconsciously begin to respect those who respect them for whatever they are. It is important that you remember this fact in dealing with people in career and personal life.

In the office or home when you greet everyone with a "good morning" and a genuine smile and courteousness, you are creating an atmosphere most conducive for mutual respect. A well respected executive is none else but the one who treats others as equal human beings, and who considers that the ego of the other person is as important as his/her own.

DON'T BRAG—LET YOUR ACTIONS SPEAK

It is a wise person who does not boast about himself/herself. It is all the more applicable for the executive in the corporate environment, where intrigues and severe competitions flourish at all levels. You will be better off keeping your motives and maneuvers secret, silently working toward your goals. It is immature to speak boastingly of what you plan to achieve and what your goals are. No body need to know them other than yourself.

Let others see you through your actions and achievements only. Actions speak louder than words and they also bring better results. Also, when you let your intentions being known beforehand you may jeopardize your own very survival and success. Your rivals among peers could counteract or make faster moves to capitalize on a favorable climate upsetting your plans. Be a person of action and not words.

DON'T BURN YOUR BRIDGES BEHIND YOU

Statistics show that the average American executive changes jobs on an average of five times in his/her life time. The chances are that you are contemplating your next move if your expected promotion or salary increase or some other benefit is not forthcoming. Changing jobs from one company to another does not always mean that you are going to a better place. There are so many reasons varying from incompatible bosses to fluctuating market conditions that may warrant a return to your old job.

For this reason it will be wise on your part not to burn the bridges behind you with the old organization. In fact, if you can keep the door open and move to the new job with the blessing of your old boss, you have little to worry. It is not uncommon to find an executive who has made a move and lost both positions in a matter of few months. Also it is not uncommon to find many executives who have returned back to their parental company after discovering in the new place the realization that they would rather be in their old jobs.

SOCIALIZE WITHOUT LOSING YOUR PERSONALITY

Socializing with bosses and fellow executives is an important aspect of an executive life. It can be by means of active games like tennis, golf, etc., or through joining the local country club as a member where one gets a chance to meet executives and professionals from other organizations. No matter what kind of socialization you do, be yourself. You don't have to fake interests and do things which are not to your liking.

Also, be extremely careful about alcoholic beverages. Remember that many a social drinker has ended up as alcoholic. If you are a teetotaller be bold to stay that way. Others, including your bosses, will respect you for your stand, though they may not express it openly. You don't have to compromise your values and personality for the sake of career interest. It is not worth it if you can not be yourself.

FOCUS ON A SPECIFIC GOAL

If there is a key to success in life, it is focus: you must have a clear goal. This principle works equally well for short range as well as long range goals. Focus implies a clear vision of what you are seeking and mobilizing all your energies towards achieving it.

When you have more than one project to work on, have the priorities established so that you can focus on the top-priority item without neglecting others. A top priority item should not be treated at a crisis level where everything else is pushed aside. Executives who treat a priority item as a crisis end up having to deal with crises continuously. They are the candidates for the so-called "stress-overload" which may affect them seriously.

Getting things done becomes easier when you focus on goals one at a time. Focusing helps to get the requisite activities leading to the goal organized for effective execution.

CHAPTER 7

EXECUTIVE PRINCIPLES OF THIRUVALLUVAR

"Learn whatever that are to be learned without doubts and distortions and after learning conduct yourself according to the principles learned."

Thiruvalluvar,
Thirukural (verse 391)

TOPICS

1. Thirukural, the Book of Ethics and Principles
2. Importance of Ethical Conduct
3. Executive Principles on Self-Excellence
4. Executive Principles on Communication
5. Executive Principles on Decision making
6. Executive Principles on Getting Ready for Action
7. Executive Principles on Personnel Selection
8. Executive Principles on Action
9. Executive Principles on The Manner of Conducting Business Affairs
10. Executive Principles on Stress Management
11. Executive Principles on Bodily Health

THIRUKURAL, THE BOOK OF ETHICS AND PRINCIPLES

Thiruvalluvar, the poet, philosopher, and saint of India lived around 300 B.C. in the present day State of Tamil Nadu in India. His poetic masterpiece, written in Tamil, called "Thirukural" is considered by scholars as the world's foremost book on principles and ethics for living and conducting the state's affairs directed to kings and ministers, who were the chief executives of the times. It also addresses citizens taken to worldly life and those who renounced this worldly life and preferred a spiritual life.

Next to the Bible, Thirukural is the only book that has been translated into almost all major languages of the world. In this chapter are presented only a few randomly selected principles for the executive which are relevant in today's business world. The serious reader is referred to the original Thirukural for a comprehensive look.

IMPORTANCE OF ETHICAL CONDUCT

Thirukural deals primarily with the mundane aspect of our living. It emphasizes not only the need for Dharma, that is ethical and moral conduct, for every one but also the need to have material wealth and love. Accordingly, it is divided into three major sections: Principles of Dharma (ethics and morals), Principles of Artha (materialism), and Principles of Kama (love). The Dharma part refers to ethics and morals for all people in general, house-holders and Sanyasi's (those who renounced this worldly life) in particular.

The second part on Materialism is the one that directly addresses the executives in detail. Principles, skills, and tactics for various situations are so skillfully intertwined and set in a simple but powerful poetic form of couplets or verses of two lines each. They are universally applicable for all human executive endeavors for male and female transcending the geographic boundaries of countries.

The third part on Love deals with the subtle expressions of human physical love at the psychological plane, unparalleled in any literature on human love.

The focal point of Thirukural always is on human nature and human behavior at its complex form. The principles presented in Thirukural prepare the executive for self-excellence first and then for the management of executive functions.

The whole book contains 1330 verses or couplets, each set in seven syllables of poetic elegance. No executive of modern times who has set his/her eyes on top-level performance can afford to overlook the principles expounded in Thirukural.

EXECUTIVE PRINCIPLES ON SELF-EXCELLENCE

On Kindness of Speech

Better even than a generous gift are sweet words and a kind and gracious look.   (Verse 92)

Modesty and loving speech alone are ornaments to a person, and none other.   (verse 95)

On Control of Tongue

Whatever else you control or not, control your tongue; for an uncontrolled tongue can lead you into grief.   (verse 127)

The burn caused by fire heals in the course of time; but the wound burned in by the tongue does not heal.   (verse 129)

On Good Conduct

The person of good conduct is honored by all; hence conduct is to be prized even above life.   (verse 131)

Good conduct becomes the seed of thankfulness, whereas an evil course of action becomes the cause of endless troubles.   (verse 138)

On Truthfulness

Truthfulness is speech that is free from even the slightest taint of ill-will.   (verse 291)

Even falsehood takes the place of truth if it brings forth unmixed good.   (verse 292)

Don't hold forth as truth what your heart knows to be false; for your own conscience will burn you when the truth comes to light.
(verse 293)

On Abstaining from Anger

It is wrong to get angry at those whom your anger can not hurt; but yet, there is nothing worse than anger where you can hurt.
(verse 302)

Is there a greater foe than anger that kills the smile and destroys cheer? (verse 304)

If you want to look after yourself, control your anger; for if you don't it will destroy you. (verse 305)

On Continuous Learning

Acquire thoroughly the knowledge that is worth acquiring; and after acquiring it conduct yourself in accordance therewith.

(verse 391)

Deeper you dig, more water the sand-spring yields; the more you learn, the more will be your knowledge. (verse 396)

Learning to a person is an imperishable and flawless treasure; other wealth is nothing before it. (verse 400)

On Listening to the Wise

The most precious of treasures is the treasure of the ear; it is the crown among all wealth. (verse 411)

Listen to the good words of the wise though they be but few; even those few words will bring you great honor and dignity. (verse 416)

Humility of speech is hard to be attained by those who have not listened to the subtle words of the wise. (verse 419)

EXECUTIVE PRINCIPLES ON COMMUNICATION

On Use of Kind Words

It is Dharma (the highest ethical principle) to look kindly at the face of a person with a smile on your face and to speak gentle words that spring from the heart. (verse 93)

The words that do not deviate from the goodness of heart create friendship and goodwill and bring forth benefits. (verse 97)

How can a person continue to use arrogant and unkind words, even after he has enjoyed the sweetness that kind words give.

(verse 99)

On Avoiding Gossip

Utterance of useless words in front of others is worse than doing unfriendly deeds to one's own best friend. (verse 192)

If persons of good reputation engage in useless gossip they will lose their respect and credibility.   (verse 195)

On Eloquence of Verbal communication

Prosperity and ruin are in the power of the tongue; therefore, guard yourself against imprudence of speech.   (verse 642)

It is speech that can bring those who listen closer to you and it can soften the hearts of even enemies.   (verse 643)

Choose your words such that no other word can excel.

(verse 645)

The characteristics of a good communicator is to speak in such a way as to bind the listeners to himself, and he, in turn, absorbs the substance in the words of others.   (verse 646)

The person who is eloquent of speech and unafraid of the assembly is hard to defeat in debate.   (verse 647)

On Face Reading

Take the person into your team at any cost who can judge a man's intentions from his looks.   (verse 703)

What is the specialty of the eye among the organs of sense if it can not assess the intentions of the heart from the face? (verse 705)

As the mirror reflects what is next to it, the face reveals the surging emotions of the mind.   (verse 706)

What is there that is subtler than the face? for whether the heart is angry or happy it is the face that expresses it first.   (verse 707)

Those who can understand the communication of the eye alone can sense the hatred and friendship in the hearts of men. (verse 709)

EXECUTIVE PRINCIPLES ON DECISION MAKING

Decide upon any action only after careful deliberation; it is foolish to jump into action saying that he will think afterwards. (verse 467)

Don't begin any operation except after making a thorough reconnaissance of the theater of operation.   (verse 491)

Get a full picture of the difficult nature of the operation, your own strength, the strength of your adversary, and also the strength of your allies before starting on the venture.   (verse 471)

Even the delicate feathers of a peacock can break the axle of the wagon, if you load too many of them.   (verse 475)

It does not matter if the in-flow channel is narrow, provided the out-flow channel is not wider.   (verse 478)

There is fault even in rendering a good deed to a person, if it is not done according to the human nature of the recipient. (verse 469)

Listen to the good words of the wise though they be but few; even those few words will bring you great honor and dignity. (verse 416)

If the executive decides and acts based on his emotions without consulting his good advisors, his fortunes will begin to shrink.

(verse 568)

Start on a venture only after considering the possible losses and gains in the beginning of the operation and also the profits in the long run.   (verse 461)

The wise do not encourage any venture that promises undue profit at a greater risk of losing the capital.   (verse 463)

The action which is not carried out through fair and just means will eventually fail even if it is protected by many.   (verse 468)

Think twice and decide before acting on the ventures which do not have the approval of the wise.   (verse 470)

EXECUTIVE PRINCIPLES ON GETTING READY FOR ACTION

On Knowledge

To be able to distinguish the truth from the false in the words of others, whomsoever they may be, is true knowledge.   (verse 423)

The man of knowledge knows what is coming; but the fool can not see it.   (verse 427)

It is folly to rush headlong into danger; it is wisdom to fear what ought to be feared.   (verse 428)

To the man of foresight who is armed with knowledge for every contingency there is no sudden crisis.   (verse 429)

On Self-Correction

Guard yourself against weaknesses for they are the foes that lead you to ruin.   (verse 434)

The life of the person who does not anticipate and provide for beforehand will be ruined like a stack of straw before a spark of fire.
(verse 435)

Do not vainly boast anytime; do not undertake activities that would bring you no good.   (verse 439)

On Deliberation before Action

Take into consideration the output, the wastage, and the profit that an undertaking will yield; and then apply yourself to it. (verse 461)

There are enterprises that tempt with a great profit but which perish even with the capital itself; the wise do not undertake them.
(verse 463)

There are things that ought not to be done and if you do them you will be ruined; and there are things that ought to be done and if you don't do them you will be ruined also.   (verse 466)

Decide upon any action only after careful deliberation; it is foolish to jump into action saying that he will think afterwards. (verse 467)

On Judging Self-Strength before Action

Weigh justly the difficulty of the enterprise, your own strength, the strength of your competitor, and also the strength of your allies; and then get into it.   (verse 471)

If you load too many of them even the delicate feathers of the peacock would break the wagon's axle.   (verse 475)

Those that have climbed to the top of the tree will lose their lives if they attempt to climb still higher.   (verse 476)

It does not matter if the in-flow channel is narrow, provided the out-flow channel is not wider.   (verse 478)

On Judging the Opportune Moment

Is there anything that is impossible if you start on the enterprise with a knowledge of the right time and employ the proper means?
(verse 483)

You can conquer the whole world if you choose the proper time and place to launch your operation.   (verse 484)

If you happen to get an unusual chance, that is the right time for quick action.   (verse 489)

When the time is against you feign inaction like the stork; but when the tide is on, act with the swiftness of the stork's strike.

(verse 490)

On Judging the Theater of Operation

Don't begin any operation except after making a thorough reconnaissance of the theater of operation.   (verse 491)

The plans of your adversaries will be baffled if you fall back on strong positions already reconnoitered and base yourself on them.

(verse 494)

All-powerful is the crocodile in deep waters; but out of water it is no match for its foes.   (verse 495)

EXECUTIVE PRINCIPLES ON PERSONNEL SELECTION

On Selecting Right Personnel

If you scrutinize closely, it is rare to find people without faults even among the highly educated.   (verse 503)

Weigh a person's good, as well as his evil; whichever is predominant, take that to be his nature.   (verse 504)

One's own conduct is the touchstone of one's character that reveals his noble qualities and little-mindedness.   (verse 505)

If you choose a fool for your confidential advisor just because you like him, he will lead you to endless follies.   (verse 507)

Never trust people without trying them; and after trying them, give each one of them the work for which he is fit.   (verse 509)

To trust a person whom you have not tried, and to suspect a person who has been tried and found worthy will bring alike endless ills.

(verse 510)

On Appointing Right Persons to the Right Job

Look for the person who chooses the good of things after looking at their good and bad sides; take him into your service.   (verse 511)

Select that person for your service who is endowed with kindness, intelligence, decisiveness, and greedlessness.   (verse 513)

Be aware that there are many men who satisfy every test but yet falter in the actual performance of duty.   (verse 514)

Work should be entrusted to persons in consideration of their expert knowledge and capacity for patient exertion, and not of their love for you.   (verse 515)

Look for the skilled person and give him the work for which he is fit; let him begin when the time is ripe for performance. (verse 516)

Ascertain first whether the person is capable of completing the job with the available means, and then leave him in responsible charge of the project.   (verse 517)

After you have decided that a person is fit for an office, raise him to the status and give him the authority that will enable him to fill that office in a worthy manner.   (verse 518)

You will be a loser if you misunderstand the liberties taken by this person in the discharge of his duties who is skillful and honest at his work.   (verse 519)

Let the Chief Executive Officer oversee everything everyday; for nothing can go wrong with the enterprise so long as there is nothing wrong with the officers under him.   (verse 520)

EXECUTIVE PRINCIPLES ON ACTION

On Attentiveness

Nothing is impossible to the person who can bring into his work a mind that is ever wakeful and cautious.   (verse 537)

It is not difficult for a person to achieve all that he desires, provided he keeps his purpose constantly before his mind.   (verse 540)

On Energy and Enthusiasm

Energy and enthusiasm alone can be called a person's true wealth; for riches do not endure for ever and will depart from him one day.
(verse 592)

The men that hold in their hands the resource called unremitting energy will never despair saying "Alas, we lost all our wealth".
(verse 593)

Good fortune inquires its way to the home of the person who is endowed with unshakable energy and enthusiasm.   (verse 594)

Men of spirit do not lose their heart when they meet with defeat; the elephant in the battle field plants its legs only more firmly when he is hit by the deep piercing arrow.   (verse 597)

The men that are wanting in energy and enthusiasm can never achieve success and glory in this world.   (verse 598)

On Abstaining from Procrastination & Laziness

Procrastination, forgetfulness, laziness, and oversleep, these are the four cozy pleasure boats of those that are destined to perish.   (verse 605)

The lazy can never reach the pinnacle of success in their endeavors even though they may have the favor of kings.   (verse 606)

The misfortunes that may have befallen a man's family will cease to exist the moment he gives up laziness.   (verse 609)

On Hard Work

Beware of leaving any work unfinished; for the world does not care for those who do not complete the work that they have once begun.   (verse 612)

The man who does not love pleasure but loves work is a pillar of strength unto his friends and he will be able to remove their grief.   (verse 615)

Hard work brings prosperity; but laziness brings only poverty and destitution.   (verse 616)

It is no shame if a man is not favored by fortune; but it is a disgrace if he abstains deliberately from hard work.   (verse 618)

Even when the Gods don't seem to favor, sincere hard work is bound to pay the wages of labor.   (verse 619)

On Decisive Action

Greatness of achievement is nothing else but the greatness of will behind the action; all other things do not count.   (verse 661)

There are two guiding principles of the wise: one is to avoid all action that is bound to fail and the other is not to turn away from one's purpose because of obstacles.   (verse 662)

To say a thing is easy for any man; but it is rare indeed to get it done the manner in which it was said.   (verse 664)

The man who has acquired a reputation as a man of action by doing great deeds will be esteemed by all; his services will be greatly in request by kings.   (verse 665)

Whatever you desire you will achieve if you have the will and determination.   (verse 666)

Do not think low of a person by his appearance; for there are men who are like the axle-pin of the mighty rolling car.   (verse 667)

When you have undertaken a mission go after it without fear or misgiving; but with vigor and enthusiasm.   (verse 668)

EXECUTIVE PRINCIPLES ON THE MANNER OF CONDUCTING BUSINESS AFFAIRS

Even under extreme stress, the upright executive will not undertake illegal activities.   (verse 654)

Undertake those activities that bear good results in the end, even if they cause a lot of difficulties in the beginning.   (verse 669)

The end of all deliberations is to arrive at a decision; and when a decision is made it is wrong to delay the execution thereof.
                    (verse 671)

Do with deliberation those things that ought to be done in a slow pace; but don't delay those things that require prompt action.
                    (verse 672)

Go straight for the goal whenever circumstances permit; but when circumstances are against, follow the path of least resistance.
                    (verse 673)

Unfinished work and unsubdued enemies are like unextinguished sparks of fire; they will grow in time and bring havoc.   (verse 674)

Five things should be carefully considered in undertaking a mission: the resources on hand, the available equipments, the nature of the action itself, the proper time, and place for its execution.
                    (verse 675)

Carefully consider the goal, the obstacles on the way, and the expected profit before taking up an enterprise.   (verse 676)

The way to succeed in any undertaking is to learn the secret thereof by gaining the acceptance of the man who is an expert in it.
(verse 677)

Men decoy one elephant by means of another; even so make one enterprise the means of achieving a second.   (verse 678)

EXECUTIVE PRINCIPLES ON STRESS MANAGEMENT

When you are under stress, smile; for there is nothing like a smile to overcome stress.   (verse 621)

A whole sea of troubles will abase themselves the moment the man of knowledge faces them with courage and fortitude.(verse 622)

The man who is prepared to strain his every nerve like the bull to wade through every difficulty will be able to break through the stressful situations.   (verse 624)

If you develop the attitude of even-mindedness and do not rejoice unduly at your fortunes, you will not be unduly stressed in your misfortunes.   (verse 626)

The wise know that the body is the target of mental stress; and so they do not allow themselves to be overcome by stress and grief.
(verse 627)

The man who does not run after pleasure and who knows that difficulties are part of the law of mundane life does not come to grief.
(verse 628)

The person who does not run after pleasure in days of success does not come to grief in days of failure.   (verse 629)

EXECUTIVE PRINCIPLES ON BODILY HEALTH

On Abstaining from Alcohol

Those who are addicted to alcohol will not be feared by their enemies and they will lose whatever respect they have had before from others.   (verse 921)

Do not drink alcohol; drink it if you don't care for the esteem of worthy men.   (verse 922)

Drinking alcohol is no different from drinking poison; nor are the alcoholics different from the dead and from those asleep. (verse 925)

The addicts who drink alcohol in secret will soon be found by the people around and will be held in utter contempt.   (verse 927)

While being sober, when the alcoholic sees the drunken state of another man, can he not picture to himself his own state when he is drunk?   (verse 930)

On the Right Food

The body requires no medicine if food is taken only after the previously eaten meal is fully digested.   (verse 942)

Eat the proper quantity of food after the previous meal is digested; that is the secret of longevity.   (verse 943)

Wait till the previous meal is 'digested fully and your appetite becomes keen; then eat moderately the food that agrees with your system.   (verse 944)

If you eat your food in moderation that is acceptable to your system, then you will have no troubles in the body.   (verse 945)

As good health stays with the man who eats only when his stomach is empty, even so disease stays with him who eats to excess.

(verse 946)

One who is ignorant and gluttonous and eats more food than needed to appease his hunger will become sick beyond measure.

(verse 947)

PART 3

STRESS, HEALTH, & PERFORMANCE

CHAPTER 8

EXECUTIVE STRESS MANAGEMENT

"To those who have the wisdom to anticipate, plan beforehand, and act there is no shocking crisis in life".

Thiruvalluvar
Thirukural (verse 429)

TOPICS

1. Executive Stress
2. Sources of Executive Stress
3. People Management
4. Time Management
5. Mobility
6. Promotions and Adjustments
7. Performance and Self-Doubt
8. The Race to the Top
9. Personal Financial Management
10. Family Problems
11. Incompatible Goals
12. Success Syndrome—the Stress of Success
13. What to Do Now, Reaching the Top?

EXECUTIVE STRESS

Stress is a non-specific response of individuals to the environment. This environment includes people, place, and situations with which the executive interacts in his/her daily life. No two people respond the same way to a given stressor. Stress is not always bad. What is stressful to one may even be invigorating to another.

Stress does not kill, but stress response can. That is, when the stress moves from the psyche (mind) plane to the somatic (body) plane, it can affect the bodily functions such as sleep, digestion, blood circulation, and nervous system negatively and disturb the homeostasis of the body. The symptoms of stress are unmistakable: sleeplessness, headaches, fatigue, nervous tension, mood changes, etc.

Unmanaged stress is like unregulated flood which can break through the banks and do more harm than good. Unmanaged stress, when allowed to persist over a long period of time, can result in a multitude of psychosomatic illnesses, of which stomach ulcers, hypertension (high blood pressure), cardiovascular and renal problems are but a few to mention.

Stress is not something to be afraid of or unduly concerned about. It is part of being human, more so being an executive. There is no such thing as life without stress, occupation without tension, or career without problems. It is a matter of learning to cope with them. Executives who have chosen organizational life, of course, must be competitive to achieve competence for effective job performance. No doubt, the need to compete and achieve is highly stressful for many of them, and those who can not manage do suffer impairment of health.

Harry Levinson, in his book "Executive Stress", mentions "executives most often do not differentiate between creative and self-destructive competitiveness. They assume that if they have chosen organizational life, the inevitable product is stress and they will have to take their chances, worrying all the way and unable to do anything about it. It isn't and they won't".

There is no need for the executives to resign to the notion that sooner or later stress is going to get them. Stress is manageable when you understand the cause and effect relationship and discipline yourself to spend some time and effort to counteract the stress preventively and curatively. Also, you will be able to use stress as a motivator for your achievement and advancement in career.

SOURCES OF EXECUTIVE STRESS

Stress for the executive can arise from career or personal life or both. The major sources of executive stress are:

- People management
- Time management
- Mobility
- Promotions and adjustments
- Performance and self-doubt
- The race to the top
- Personal financial management
- Family problems
- Incompatible goals
- Success syndrome—the stress of success

PEOPLE MANAGEMENT

The foremost source of stress for most executives lies in their interpersonal relations. The ability to interact with others—bosses, peers, subordinates and others in the office environment with a reasonable degree of confidence without being or becoming uncomfortable shapes up the executive behavior. It is so unique for each individual it can not just be listed as a skill to acquire; each person has to come to grip with this phenomenon through conscious effort to improve oneself. To that degree of ease with which an executive can deal with people at all levels, he/she will be less stressed. Effectiveness in people management is discussed under Reinforcer Skills in Chapter 3.

TIME MANAGEMENT

The second major source of stress for the executive lies in his/her ability to manage time. Unlike other resources, time is an irrecoverable entity which can only be spent or wasted. Achievement of results and performance are directly related to his/her ability to getting things done and utilizing time well apportioned to all required activities—

executive and personal. The techniques of personal time management discussed in Chapter 3 are very effective in reducing stress for the executive when the concept of time and activity is properly applied.

MOBILITY (DISLOCATION & RELOCATION)

It is estimated that the average American executive makes five moves in a his/her career life time, often involving relocating the family. Every time a move is made, many changes and decisions need to be made such as selling the old house, buying a new one, community to live in, new church, new school for children, spouse's career interests, etc.

They have to learn to build life around the concept of mobility and transiency. They can not count on community support as non-transient families do. They have to make new friends each time they move—which can be particularly stressful for younger children in the family who have to cope with adjusting to new schools and new community. Moving can pose serious problems if the spouses have different professional and personal interests. There is no easy solution to these problems. It is, of course, stressful to everybody involved. They have to make compromises for the sake of common good which is the only way to manage stress under these circumstances.

PROMOTIONS AND ADJUSTMENTS

Everyone will generally be delighted with a promotion, but oddly enough, promotions could spell stress for many people and even "failure" for some. Promotions involve new job functions which the promotee has yet to master and perform in ways and means satisfactory to his bosses. The new job functions could be anything from a partial to total shift in his/her methods of dealing with people to acquiring new skills and knowledge not necessarily in his/her area of expertise.

Psychologically speaking, a person should not accept a promotion which requires him/her to behave in ways which are quite different from the manner in which he/she customarily prefers to act. Monetary consideration should not be the major factor in accepting a promotion.

Levinson lists the following four conditions for accepting a new position which should:

1. Permit a person to maintain his/her preferred emotional distance from others.

2. Allow him/her to use his/her characteristic ways of expressing aggression.
3. Be congenial with his/her established ways of handling his/her dependency needs.
4. Increase a person's positive feelings about himself/herself.

When a promotion is accepted after due consideration of the above-mentioned factors and with a positive attitude to put in the best effort to match the organizational and personal goals, one can be expected to be successful in the new position; the stress due to promotion will wear away soon. Otherwise, the promotion can induce more stress than he/she had before.

PERFORMANCE AND SELF-DOUBT

Appraisal and evaluation of individual performance in the executive position is a stressful event· for most people. Various means are employed by the employer to assess the performance with a view to have an idea of how well the executive is functioning in his/her position. Since salary rises and promotions are generally tied to effectiveness of performance, any body is naturally concerned about their own performance. This concern can be highly stressful when the executive nurtures self-doubt.

Self-doubt arises from a person's feeling that he/she is not as good or as strong as he/she thinks. It is an aggravated feeling of inadequacy stemming from one's own conscience. Fear of failure at the subconscious level of the mind nurtures self-doubt. It is a feeling that executives understand least because so many of them deny their own fears and push such feelings our of their consciousness.

Many executives have been pushed to great heights of achievements by self-doubt as a way of proving themselves in their own eyes and in the eyes of others. On the other hand, self-doubt can hold people back from putting their best efforts which they are capable of.

Self-doubt, or lack of self-confidence, is the single most important factor that affects the job performance of most executives, though well qualified and experienced. He/she is unable to trust himself/herself to undertake a greater responsibility for which he is qualified and capable. He/she is more constricted and inhibited by his/her own fears than by objective limitations.

What can the executive do to extricate himself/herself from the grips of self-doubt?

- The first step is to recognize that self-doubt is a normal and natural feeling for all human beings.
- The second step is to have faith in your potential for self-efforts and achievements, and start applying yourself to the tasks on hand with fervor and enthusiasm.
- Without worrying about how you are doing, keep working enjoying what you are doing.

Therein lies the secret of effective performance.

THE RACE TO THE TOP

Executives in general aspire to move towards the top-most position of the organization. The race to the top through the corporate hierarchy is not on a smooth track. Upward mobility itself is a disruptive social experience which tends to leave the individual for an appreciable period without roots or effective social support. A person who cherishes family life is torn apart when he/she must sacrifice family relationships for career goals.

There are other unpleasant experiences. If a young executive believes that job performance and hard work alone are needed for success, he/she will be angered when he/she finds that political maneuvering, favoritism, and nepotism are rewarded often even at the expense of sincerity at work.

Rapid upward mobility may also mean repetitive breaking of old attachments—from the world of the family to jobs, colleagues, activities, locations, and often even a professional skill as well. Chances of making new friends outside of career milieu decrease due to want of time. Often spending enough time with spouse and children at home becomes a luxury for the too-success-conscious executive.

The failure to move up, on the other hand, constitutes another source of stress. Apart from limitations of his/her own competence, there are two major road blocks to upward mobility: one is his/her being side-tracked onto less important assignments and the other is being stuck behind superiors who are not moving.

Young executives with pressing aspirations will tend to become impatient with such blocks. Impatience leads to frustration which, in turn, turns into anger. If the executive is not aware of the ways to deal with it, anger can become internalized and reflect itself in tension, irritability, or other psychosomatic manifestations.

The fact that the race to the top is not smooth and that it is studded with stresses of all kinds does not necessarily imply that it is not worth striving at. By knowing what is ahead the executive can be better prepared to handle the stresses along the route. With all the thorns surrounding it, a rose is still a worthy target to pluck at for one who desires it.

PERSONAL FINANCIAL MANAGEMENT

Though it is generally believed that executives are better equipped to manage their own finances, it is not the case with so many of them. Stress researchers have observed that poor personal financial management is often a source of severe stress for them, which severely affects them adversely in their job performance. Few people realize that just by earning "a lot" of money , one does not automatically solve all his/her financial problems. They also don't realize that there are principles to understand and follow in the handling of money once it is lawfully earned.

Considering the nature of their all-time validity, the seven principles of personal financial management are given below regardless of their seeming simplicity:

1. Budget your expenses
2. Save with objectives
3. Invest with objectives
4. Protect your investment
5. Provide for home ownership
6. Provide for your retirement years
7. Explore further avenues of income.

Budget Your Expenses

Spending for needs within the available income is the first principle of financial management. The tool for this is a budget. A monthly budget can regulate your expenditures in a controlled manner, providing for your needs and limited luxuries. The various items of a personal budget may vary for each individual, but the principle of balancing the budget within the available income is still the same.

It is worth recalling the words of Thiruvalluvar written more than two thousand years ago: "It does not matter if the flow of income is small, provided that the outflow channel is not wider. (verse 478). The life of a person who does not live within the bounds of his income, though appearing prosperous, will be ruined leaving no trace behind. (verse 479)".

Save with Objectives

Developing a positive attitude towards saving and including a systematic provision in your monthly budget for savings towards meaningful objectives are vital for sound financial management. It will pave the way for better living. The reasons for saving can be listed in three major categories:

1. To create investment reserves,
2. To meet emergency needs, and
3. To meet non-routine expenses such as a vacation, etc.

David West and Glenn Wood, authors of "Personal Financial Management", state that the failure to build up a savings fund is a serious financial mistake. Having a solid savings reserve to fall back on is indispensable for one's financial freedom.

Invest with Objectives

Assets create income, and learning to acquire assets in life will help you improve your financial position. Of course, your ability to earn an income is your most important asset, which you can improve through acquiring additional educational and technical skills. In effect, you are investing your natural resources of time and effort to acquire them.

In addition, there are other investments you should consider which can bring you financial returns. They include:

1. Real estate (physical assets),
2. Stocks and bonds (financial assets), and
3. Franchises and the like (intangible assets).

Protect Your Investments

It is not enough to simply invest in whatever form of assets you have chosen; it is important that you should be constantly examining their soundness and validity. The disposal of unsound assets and reinvestment in better ones should be done diligently and with care on a continuing basis. Market trends, socio-political and technological impact, and other risk factors must be taken into consideration as well. It will be wise to turn to experts for advice in matters that may be too complicated for you in the world of financial investments.

Provide for Home Ownership

If you are young you may not fully realize the importance of this step in personal financial management. Owning a home is not just an American dream, but it is a major factor in career and life planning. Home ownership increases financial security, improves one's credit standing, encourages objective saving, provides an identity to the owner, and above all contributes to better citizenship and a sense of pride. It helps meet the distant future with less stress.

Provide for Retirement Years

Though the retirement may seem quite far away for the young executive, it is a wise person who realizes the importance of starting a retirement program at an early age. When you start investing early in retirement income, you get all the advantages of the power of compound interest over a long period of time.

Explore Further Avenues of Income

The seventh principle requires that you constantly explore additional avenues of income flow. It may be through acquiring new educational and technical skills by attending graduate school, specialized skill development seminars and evening classes, by "moon-lighting" in a part-time job, or by starting a business venture cashing on a hobby skill that you might possess. The additional income generated means more money for personal enjoyments or for new investments.

The reader is referred to George Clason's book "Richest Man in Babylon" for a fascinating illustration of the principles discussed above.

FAMILY PROBLEMS

Job performance of the executive can be severely impaired when he/she has family problems, and it will be wise on his/her part to try to resolve them as early as possible with the help of counselors, if need be. Psychosomatically, the effect of stress is the same whether it originates at home or office.

Alcoholism of a spouse, chronic ill-health of a family member, conflicting career interests of husband and wife, and family financial problems are but a few typical problems that can be very stressful to the executive. There is no easy or standard solution to family problems. Each family has to work out their solutions to suit their needs and interests. Though the problems may not be fully resolved in all cases, a conscious attempt to bring them to manageable level is the goal of preventive stress management.

INCOMPATIBLE GOALS

Stress is inevitable whenever the goals of the employing organization and those of the individuals employed are not compatible. For example, take the case of an organization which has its goals limited to serve only the local and regional needs. If its executive has ambitious goals of serving at the international level, then there exists a conflict of goals which will be a constant source of stress for the executive. Either he/she has to redefine his/her goals to suit the company's or quit the organization and seek different pastures where he/she has more chances to reach for this goals.

For Women Executives and Professionals

Women executives and professionals, particularly between the ages of 30 and 36 have been known to have severe conflicts between career success on one hand and the natural desire for marriage and family on the other. Motherhood and the desire to bear children is a natural impulse in women which may become a threat to career success for ambitious women executives. Abandoning one or the other appears to be the logical step in resolving the crisis.

However, this is possible only for strong-willed individuals, and for those who could bring about a change in their attitude towards their future life. But, for those women, who couldn't decide but continue to be in the career game, severe stress is inevitable as result of harboring incompatible goals. It is not uncommon for some of them to suffer a major depression as they climb up the career ladder successfully.

It should also be noted that there are many women executives who have successfully balanced their life's interests and instincts between a career and family without being victimized by stress of conflicting goals.

SUCCESS SYNDROME—THE STRESS OF SUCCESS

Success syndrome refers to the positive and negative outcomes that follow the attainment of a significant achievement, victory or goal. Steven Berglas, in his book "Success Syndrome", refers to the devastating potential of success which can bring about severe attitudinal and behavioral changes.

The significant negative changes that can come on a highly successful executive following significant achievements in attaining prestige, power or money are:

1. Self-alienation due to non-trust
2. Self-doubt
3. Self-handicapping through alcohol abuse
4. Cognitive distortion: "I am above the law"
5. Marital moral turbidity.

Self-Alienation due to Non-Trust

"It is lonely at the top" is a common assertion by many executives who climbed to the top in a pyramid of hierarchy. They seldom realize that the loneliness is self-induced. Old friends, former peers and colleagues, even family members seem to move farther away. Though to some extent the old relationship may not be the same, it is the attitude change of the executive who puts himself/herself on a pedestal with a touch of Narcism that is responsible for the wall of aloofness that slowly crystallizes around the executive.

The process of this happening is so subtle that the executive begins to view the change as if it is coming from others. It is similar to the visionary illusion of trees running away from the person riding a high-speed train.

Self-alienation is undoubtedly a severe stress. It robs the executive of the moral strength and support which were once provided by his/her former personal contacts. The money, power, and perks that come in the wake of success can not solve his/her problem of loneliness.

The solution, though, lies in the self-realization of the executive that he is as much a human being as anybody else is and that his success does not make him superior in any sense. He/she may come to possess more material goods by virtue of the success than before. It is for him to reach out to his former friends and colleagues to show that he hasn't changed.

Self-Doubt

The performance called upon the executive during the race to the top and that after having reached the top are evaluated under different criteria; the gear is changed for the wheel. Unfortunately, most executives can not distinguish the difference and they continue to self-evaluate their own performance at the level that won them the top-position. "Having reached the top, now what?" is a question for which not all executives have the answer.

As a result, self-doubt begins to creep into their minds: "Will I be as successful as I used to be?". Once the self-doubt about one's own performance capability begins to dawn, the self-confidence of the executive is slowly eroded, and stress symptoms begin to show up.

Self-Handicapping through Alcohol Abuse

The inability of the executive to handle self-doubt seems to encourage him/her to turn to alcohol abuse. Alcohol is an effective handicapper for the user. It shields the person from insecurity and doubt about being successful and creates a temporary route of escapism. Berglas mentions that the purpose of self-handicapping is to defend a favorable but tenuous image of competency against the threats posed by periodic evaluations or assessments of ability.

Cognitive Distortion—"I am above the Law"

A frequent corruption of the mind that takes place for seemingly normal executives and others who achieve great successes and positions of power is to consider themselves invincible. They begin to believe in it once others begin to show their respect for their status, power, position or money. Psychologists call this phenomenon "cognitive distortion". Indeed, it is their distorted perception and value system towards the world around them in which they were a normal element just like anybody else before the success. Arrogance in behavior and belligerence of words are symptoms of this form of corruption. Cognitive distortion frees them from guilt feelings in matters related to the distorted notion and they tend to become insensitive to the feelings of others.

The Dark Side of Success

With the onset of cognitive distortion, the person believes that he/she is above the law which is meant for "others". Seemingly endless against-law activities of people who have reached great heights of achievements stem from their very successes, the achievements which needed the law to succeed. It is a paradox that you need a clear mind to achieve success, and the success can corrupt the very mind that made it possible!

Respect Legal, Moral, and Ethical Principles

It may appear ridiculous to suggest to an executive that he/she should respect legal, moral, and ethical principles; but, when you consider the nature of the executive powers and functions and the environment they work it is not ridiculous at all. In fact, there is a need to remind ourselves time and again some of the basic principles of human behavior such as legality, morality, and ethics for our own good and for the good of the world we live in.

The law of the land takes precedence over everything else. It is essential that all executive decisions must fall within the framework of the law. Moral issues are concerned with right and wrong and can be highly individualistic. What one person considers right can be thought of as wrong by another person. In matters of controversy follow the dictates of your own conscience; and that is moralistic for you.

Marital Moral Turbidity

Yet another trouble from success, for some who have climbed to great heights of achievements, seems to attack the cherished views of marriage and morals. Extra-marital affairs in the wake of great success have been observed by psychologists which are not isolated instances.

Though it is unwise to try to pinpoint or assign a reason for this phenomenon, it can not be equated with all other extra-marital affairs.

One explanation is that the value-system of the successful person regarding marriage falls flat and he/she wants to try on a new partner who sees him/her only through the image of success. The shaken-up value-system becomes turbid and begins to recrystallize in the presence of success for that individual. Of course, the price has to be paid for the actions in terms of family stress.

WHAT TO DO NOW, REACHING THE TOP?

It is important to remember that success is a process involving both the pursuit of a goal and the end product of achieving it. Both should be enjoyable to the goal-seeker. Once a goal is achieved, and if there are no new goals and challenges placed before the mind, routine work can bring boredom, self-doubts, and eventually stress. This is the plight of many top level executives.

"Something to do, and something to look forward to" is the common sense approach that is most appropriate in infusing new enthusiasm into the lives of those who begin to slip from success. Diversification of interests to include varied new goals and self-challenges is the logical answer for those who have reached the top. It is imperative that they keep the person as a human being separate from the cloak of success that is temporarily thrown on the person.

CHAPTER 9

EXECUTIVE HEALTH

"As good health stays with the man who eats only when his stomach is empty, even so disease stays with him who eats to excess".

Thiruvalluvar,
Thirukural (verse 946)

TOPICS

1. Meditation—Prelude to Physical Health
2. Visualization
3. Executive Uses of Visualization
4. Physical Health
5. Balanced Fitness Program
6. Heart and Blood Pressure
7. Aerobic, Yoga, and Other Exercises
8. Balanced Diet
9. Alcohol
10. Smoking
11. Hobbies
12. Vacation

MEDITATION—PRELUDE TO PHYSICAL HEALTH

Mind-body partnership is an important factor in the pursuit of good health and is the basis for holistic health programs designed for executives and others. Relaxed mind relaxes the muscles of the body, and an agitated mind tenses the body muscles. To induce relaxation in the mind the tensed muscles of the body needs to be relaxed first. Meditation as a technique is a powerful aid to pursue and maintain good physical health.

The word "meditation" means different things to different people, and to many it brings a notion of mysticism and religious and spiritual involvement of some kind. It may mean all types of normal thought processes under the conscious control of the person, such as pondering, reflecting on, contemplating, planning or projecting in the mind, etc.

Meditation also implies that the thought process is taken beyond the realm of emotions so that the thought process is not clouded by one's emotions. Because of the absence of emotions during meditation, the brain wave pattern falls, in general, in the alpha range (7 to 13 cycles per second) indicating a state of deep relaxation of the body and mind, known as the alpha state.

Many forms and levels or stages of meditation are possible along with different levels of mental awareness. Dreaming, visualization, auto-suggestion, hypnosis, religious meditation, transcendental meditation and cosmic meditation are indicative of the different possible levels of conscious awareness, which the practitioner is capable of experiencing. Hence, meditation is also known as "the experiencing experience".

Place and Time for Meditation

Though meditation can be done literally at any place, it is desirable that you practice meditation in the privacy of your home or office away from the gaze of other people or in temples of worship meant for prayer and meditation. The concern here is primarily your physical safety, because during meditation your consciousness may tend to shift way from your immediate environment for a prolonged period of time, and as such you may become oblivious to any approaching danger.

Hence, it is important that you ensure maximum safety to your person by choosing an appropriate place.

Central to meditation is an alert mind. Your choice of time for meditation should, therefore, be such that you will be able to stay awake and alert, depending on your nature of routines of daily living. Early morning and late evening hours are most suitable. Meditation should not be done within two hours of any heavy meal for obvious reasons of avoiding drowsiness and falling asleep. Though meditation does not require any special clothing, loose fitting garments to ensure maximum physical comfort and to keep you warm enough in your chosen environment are recommended.

Meditation involves turning your attention from the external environment towards your inner awareness and turning your mind to reach harmony with your inner forces. Hence, a quiet place with least external stimuli in the form of noise, smell, and other disturbances is the most desirable. Mild incense has been found to soothe the neurocenter of the brain and induce physical relaxation, the prerequisite for meditation. It is important that your meditation site is well ventilated without being unduly warm or cold.

It is also important that your family members should respect your need to be alone during the meditative period and cooperate with you in keeping a quiet environment. it is recommended that you try to adhere strictly to the meditative practice carried out at the same time and place every day as a matter of self-discipline, if not for anything else.

Procedure for Meditation

1. Choose a sitting position on the floor or in a straight-back chair that is most comfortable to you. Reclining and lying positions are not recommended for meditation as they may lead to a drowsy state of mind and sleep.
2. Having comfortably seated, pay attention to your breathing. After a couple of deep diaphragmatic breaths, return to normal breathing. Close your eyes.
3. Keep your mind in a state of passivity with no violent emotions. Thoughts provoking feelings of anger, fear, grief, or joy must not be entertained, so that you may feel fully relaxed and at ease with yourself.

4. With your eyes closed, fix your attention on the spot in your forehead between the two eye brows. You may visualize a circle with a central dot to aid in focusing your inward gaze.

5. Stay passively physically and mentally in that position—for about five minutes. Let non-emotional thoughts freely flow in your mind, keeping your inward focus on the visualized circle.

It is natural that the mind will drift from the central focus and unrelated thoughts will flow through your awareness. Do not try to force them out, nor to analyze them. Let them flow, but pull back your attention to the central focus. With continuous practice your ability to concentrate on the central focus will improve.

If you are a religious person, you can substitute an image of your religious adoration or worship at the central inner focus.

You will begin to feel the relaxation of your tensed forehead muscles as if a spring is unwinding itself slowly. You may not be able to note this subtle change in the muscle tension in the early days of practicing meditation, but very soon you will become sensitive to it.

How long you want to stay in this state of meditation is up to you. It is recommended that you spend about 20 minutes every day for meditation primarily as a relaxation technique.

VISUALIZATION

Visualization is the process of forming mentally visual images of objects or ideas not present to the physical eye. It is an imagined scene with all its concreteness of notion and clarity of details as if you see a painting on a canvas. It is most effective in the alpha state of relaxation in the meditative state when the mind is most receptive. Visualization holds the key to unlock the higher reaches of one's own consciousness.

When you create a vivid mental picture, your body actually responds to the visualization as if it were a real experience. Dr. Maxwell Maltz, author of "Psycho-cybernetics", mentions that your nervous system can not tell the difference between an imagined experience and a real experience. In either case, it acts automatically to the information you provide from your forebrain. Your nervous system reacts appropriately to what you visualize, thus establishing a psychophysical response to the visualized imagery. All religious and spiritual experiences involve visualizations of one form or other appropriate to the concepts of that religion.

EXECUTIVE USES OF VISUALIZATION

The powerful technique of visualization can be put into direct use by the executive in the following matters that concern himself/herself in personal life as well as career:

1. Self-acceptance
2. Self-psychoanalysis
3. Instant relaxation
4. Problem solving
5. Decision making.

Self-Acceptance

Self-acceptance means accepting and coming to terms with ourselves now, just as we are, with all the faults, weaknesses, shortcomings, errors, as well as assets and strengths. Dr. Maxwell Maltz wrote in his book, "Creative Living for Today",: "your surest guide to success is your acceptance of yourself".

With your eyes closed in the meditative position let your "I" consciousness project your self-image—that is "you" on your mental screen, so that you are able to see your faults, weaknesses, shortcomings, and strengths. Be honest with yourself and bring to the visualization "the real personality which you consider as yourself". This is your self-image at this point of time. Still in the meditative position, eyes closed, suggest to yourself to accept this image of yours in total in your mind. This in effect is an auto-suggestion.

The suggestion of acceptance is carried out by your subconscious mind. After about 15 minutes of meditative session open your eyes slowly. Stay relaxed for a couple of minutes before getting up and resuming your normal activities.

During your waking hours the suggestion of the subconscious begins to act on your conscious mind. Repeat the visualization of self-acceptance drama in the stage of your mind during subsequent meditative sessions till you are totally comfortable with your self-image.

Remember that psychophysical processes are very subtle and slow. It is important that you must have faith in what you are doing and keep doing meditation as a part of your daily routines.

How does self-acceptance work? Self-acceptance acts like a powerful catalyst. It makes you feel more secure within yourself. By accepting yourself as you are, you will be able to eliminate unresolved conflicts in the conscious level of your mind. Self-acceptance provides a release for the stresses which could otherwise accumulate in competitive living. Your worth as a human being increases in your eyes, thus enhancing your self-esteem. You will not say "I hate myself" any more.

Self-Psychoanalysis

Self-psychoanalysis, when properly applied, is a powerful tool at your disposal for attitude and behavior modification on your part in your behavioral pattern where conflicts exist. It is most effective after self-acceptance.

With your eyes closed in the meditative position, bring yourself to the alpha state of relaxation. Pick up one event at a time from your past behavioral history that bothers you very often. It the stage of your mind, reconstruct the same or similar event, however unpleasant and uncomfortable it may be. Visualize it in all its details. View the scene objectively as if you are viewing the performance of a movie character on the screen and evaluate yourself in the scene to know how you reacted to those past events. Note your personality traits in those incidents. Analyze them objectively and try to find which of the trait or traits in you are the cause of the conflict.

Repeat this session of visualization and analysis of the same scene till you are able to objectively identify the source of the conflict. Using this as a guide, you can take steps for suitable modifications in your attitude and behavior in the future, so that no conflict is encountered in similar events. By repeatedly going through those events in your mind in successive meditative sessions and matching them with your chosen attitude and behavior modifications, you will be able to minimize, if not entirely eliminate, the effects of the stressful conflicts.

Instant Relaxation

You can do this in your home or office. With your eyes closed in the meditative position visualize yourself as a totally relaxed person enjoying the serenity of the secluded beach on the ocean front, or any other scene which you can recall from your past experiences or recent vacation. Your nervous system gets the message and conveys to the skeletal muscles to relax as if you were on the beach or the visualized scene.

Problem Solving

You can apply visualization as an aid in career related problem solving. With your eyes closed in the meditative position, visualize the problem in its entirety and analyze all possible practical solutions. Through repeated visualization you will begin to have a better perception of the problem and the best possible solution.

Through visualization you can also analyze the implications of the proposed solution that you may tend to choose.

Decision Making

No where among the executive functions visualization is more useful to the executive than in decision making. In order for decision making to be a rational process, all related factors need to be analyzed.

Close your eyes and bring yourself to the alpha state of meditation. Visualize the issue needing decision in a Gestalt manner, that is, form a total and complete picture of the issue in your mind with all the inputs and factors. Visualize also all alternate solutions and their impact as far as you can figure out. Compare the pros and cons of the alternate solutions. Decide on the best course of action which is superior to all alternatives from the benefit and cost points of view. Repeat the same visualization for at least three sessions. If you come up with the same solution every time, then that is the one to be decided upon.

PHYSICAL HEALTH

Next to mental health nothing is more important to the executive than good physical health. Many executives take it for granted and do not pay attention to it till they start having "health problems". They do not realize that most of their so-called health problems were brought on by themselves by sheer neglect and could have been pre-vented had they paid some attention for preventive health management through a balanced fitness program.

Almost all executive and professional jobs are sedentary in nature and do not involve brisk bodily movements. The executives are always at race with the clock to meet deadlines in whatever they do. It is a continuous rat race for many to reach the top. As a result, a sense of balanced living slowly slips off from their routines.

The combination of a gradual increase in stress overload in their life style, the sedentary nature of the job, and the neglect of a system-atic physical exercise program takes a synergistic turn leading to phys-ical problems. Headaches, sleeplessness, nervous tension, ulcers, hypertension (high blood pressure), cardiovascular problems are but a few of the most common executive sicknesses.

Apart from the physical suffering they cause, they affect the job performance of the executive. The pity is that most of these illnesses are preventable through the adoption of a Balanced Fitness Program (BFP). BFP helps not only to prevent the occurrence of most of them, but also brings a sense of physical well-being which is conducive for better performance for the executive.

BALANCED FITNESS PROGRAM (BFP)

What is a Balanced Fitness Program ?

BFP is a preventive health management system designed exclu-sively for the individual based on the following **five** factors:

1. Age
2. Overall condition of the physique
3. Physical activity on the job
4. Stress level on the job
5. Personal life style.

BFP is carried out in conjunction with an appropriate diet change and regulation to match these five factors.

Though age is no bar to any exercise program, the type, intensity, and the duration of the exercises must be compatible to the age. Whereas vigorous aerobic exercises may be quite in order for the young executive in his/her thirties, some moderate form of exercises with slow rhythm are more suited for executives in their fifties and sixties.

Not all people of the same age group are physically at the same level. Some are in excellent shape, and some are not. Obviously, the same exercise program is not to be recommended for both.

The amount of physical activity on the job varies widely. Some get to walk quite a bit during the day whereas most of the executives are sedentary and do little work physically. Some executives seem to be always on their toes and under constant stress, whereas there are others who have learned the art of relaxation and use it even during the peak working time. For these obvious reasons an individually programmed exercise must take into consideration the physical activity and stress level of the executive.

Another important factor is the personal life style. There are executives who are occupied most evenings in many different activities including churches and clubs whereas there are those who keep themselves free in the evenings.

BFP aims at balancing these various factors at the individual level so that a suitable holistic exercise program can be worked out for the individual's need. It is important that you consult with your doctor for a physical check-up and work out a Balanced Fitness Program for yourself under doctor's guidance.

BFP is Holistic

The philosophy of the Balanced Fitness Program revolves on the holistic concept that a healthy mind and a healthy body compliment each other for a healthy living. The guidelines on which a BFP is based are:

1. Healthy mind
2. Healthy heart and normal blood pressure
3. Optimum body weight
4. Flat stomach.

Heart and Blood Pressure

At the very center of healthy and happy living is the heart. No other part of the body is directly pushed into action every time you experience stress as your heart. Being about the size of a fist and weighing less than a pound, the heart is perhaps the world's most wonderful machine that is built to last a life time of continuous action. Though small in size it beats an average of 72 times a minute. Every organ of the body is directly dependent of the heart for the vital supply of oxygen and nutrients necessary, which are carried though it by the blood circulation system monitored by the heart.

The heart is a pump and a muscle. It provides the driving force for the circulation of the blood through the blood vessels, and it is this fluid pressure commonly referred to as blood pressure. Each thrust of this pump is called a heart beat. Though it normally ranges from 60 and 80 per minute, under conditions of emotional stress and intense muscular exertion the heart beat rate can increase twofold. It must be noted that a healthy heart is a slow heart. A heart that can take care of the circulation needs of the body with less number of thrusts has more time to relax in between!

Optimum Body Weight

Body weight is an index of a person's health. Weight accumulates only when energy intake exceeds energy expenditure, and the possibility of this occurring is influenced by psychological, social, cultural, and genetic factors. Psychologists have found that stressed persons have a tendency to overeat. Anxiety and frustration have been known to make people seek solace in food, the consumption of which represents a pleasurable pastime. However, it may result in an undesirable gain in body weight, which medical science has long since recognized as a health hazard. Ideally, your weight should remain constant after the age of 25. Consult with your doctor to ascertain your optimum desirable weight, and use it as your standard for your Balanced Fitness Program.

Flat Stomach

Many people seem to think that as a person grows older he/she tends to lose physical shape, become flabby, and develop bulging stomachs. Nothing can be far from the truth. Not paying attention to what they eat, when they eat, and how much they eat are the main factors together with a total disregard to physical exercises that cause this malady.

A flat stomach has been found to be an index of a healthy physique at its optimum weight. Besides, it is conducive for a trim image, which all executives, male or female, would like to project.

AEROBIC, YOGA, & OTHER EXERCISES

What are the exercises that constitute the Balanced Fitness Program? On principles, any system of physical exercises—by whatever name they are called such as isometrics, isotonic, calisthenics, Hatha Yoga, etc.—is suited for BFP so along as they provide the following muscle activities:

1. Stretching
2. Flexing
3. Strengthening
4. Aerobic conditioning.

Yoga exercises are ideally suited for the first three muscle activities, but are deficient in aerobic conditioning. Aerobic conditioning is best done through fast walking, jogging, rope skipping, running-in-place, stair climbing, walking on treadmill, swimming, bicycling, etc.

Aerobic Exercises for Stress Relief

Besides being part any Balanced Fitness Program, aerobic exercises are well suited for physiological relaxation. Aerobics differ from recreation, isometrics, isotonic, and Hatha Yoga in that you pick an activity such as running and gradually over a period of several weeks build your body up so as to demand large amounts of oxygen for the sustained length of time. Aerobic exercises are those that usually can be maintained for at least 10 minutes and during the performance of which no true oxygen debt is incurred.

Dr. Kenneth Cooper developed a point system to rate various common everyday activities such as walking, jogging, running, rope skipping, stair climbing, swimming, cycling. The unique feature of this system is that it allows an individual to equate different activities in terms of energy expenditure and, in this way, to determine which kinds of activities are best suited for him/her and also how long one must participate in an activity to attain beneficial results.

For example, for an average 35 year old person, 30 minutes of walking 5 days a week or 15 minutes of rope skipping 5 days a week provide about 22 points. For this person, the same effect can be derived from 16 minutes of running 5 days a week. Earning 24 points every week is considered maintenance level for excellent physical fitness. This, incidentally, also provides physiological relaxation and relief from neuromuscular tension built up during the course of a working day.

Aerobic exercises have been known to significantly improve the cardiovascular system and at the same time develop adequate levels of the other three components of physical fitness—muscular strength, endurance, and flexibility. Because of the continuous movement and flexing of body muscles, aerobic exercises have the highest potential for physiological stress relief and relaxation. They can be performed outdoor or indoor, and they need minimum equipment, if any.

Relaxation Sports

Consult with your physician to choose the right type of sports, if you are a sport-minded person, to suit your health conditions and needs. Sports can be relaxing and also can contribute to your overall physical well-being. Highly competitive and rigorous sports must be avoided, since they may constitute a source of stress instead of providing relaxation. Activities like swimming, golf, tennis, handball, canoeing, badminton, hiking, squash, horseback riding, skating, cycling, bowling, and rowing can be physically stimulating and mentally relaxing.

Regularity of Exercises

Based on the principles of the Balanced Fitness Program, it is for you to choose and work out your own program of physical or Yoga exercises combined with an aerobic activity or a relaxation sport. No matter what your choices are, you will derive the most benefit from them only when you enjoy doing them and include them into your living pattern with a certain frequent regularity, at least three times a week or every alternate day. Such a regularity will pave the way for body conditioning and relief from residual muscle tension accumulated during the intervals.

BALANCED DIET

All physical fitness programs will be meaningful and efficacious only when you adhere to a few basic principles of good diet and nutrition for the body. Lack of understanding and control of the dietary principles and intake of food can seriously jeopardize your health. Eating is an integral part of our living. Your ideas regarding what to eat, when to eat, and how much to eat constitute an important aspect of your knowledge related to food.

Your aim should be to eat a balanced diet. A balanced diet contains adequate quantities of protein, carbohydrates, and fats—all of which provide energy. Besides it also contains vitamins, minerals, and fibers which are needed for effective body functioning. Thus a balanced diet gives you all the nutrients and energy you need, but no more. Following are some pointers to help you maintain a balanced diet, recommended by the American Medical Association:

1. Do not eat meat more than once a day. Choose fish and poultry in place of red meat, sausages and processed meat. Fish and poultry are less fattening and low in cholesterol.
2. Baking or broiling food is better than frying it. If you have to fry, use polyunsaturated oils (such as corn oil) rather than butter, lard or saturated margarine.
3. Cut down on salt and other sodium containing substances in your diet such as meat tenderizers (monosodium glutamate or MSG).
4. Get your requirement of fiber by eating plenty of leafy vegetables and fruit. Eating them raw and lightly cooked preserves the essential vitamins, which are otherwise destroyed by prolonged cooking. Another good source of fiber is potato skins.
5. Eat no more than a total of four eggs a week. Though eggs are low in saturated fat, they have a very high cholesterol content.
6. For dessert or a snack choose fresh fruit rather than cakes, cookies or puddings.

Remember that the golden rule in diet is **moderation.** Too much of anything, whether it is the number of calories you consume, or a certain kind of food, is unwise. Finally, in addition to choosing a balanced and adequate meal, it is equally important to sit down and relax at meal time and enjoy what you eat.

ALCOHOL

Relaxing?

Associating alcohol with a relaxed evening is a cherished notion for many executives. A drink or two may help to create an aura of relaxation, leaving cares and worries forgotten temporarily, and may encourage sociability. At the end of a stressful working day an unhurried drink can ameliorate some of the tensions of the day, opening the way for a relaxed dinner and relaxed evening. However, you must remember that alcohol is a drug, and any drug consumed in excess and/or at the wrong time can be harmful.

Some executives under the stressful situations turn to alcohol, believing that they can manage their problems better after a drink or two. There is nothing unhealthy about one or even two average strength drinks of hard liquor—about two ounces per day. Taken this way, alcohol can serve as a tranquilizer or relaxant and as an improver of appetite.

Problem of the Social Drinker

However, the world of alcohol is very deceptive, and it drags in many a so-called "social drinker" into a state of dependence on alcohol slowly without his/her being aware of it. What happens is that the cells of the body accommodate the presence of alcohol and their tolerance level increases. Due to this increased tolerance the drinker has to take an increased quantity of alcohol to provide the same effect as before, trying to relax himself/herself—unaware of the continuously increasing alcohol content in his/her blood circulation.

Most of the alcohol in the body is handled by the liver, and as such most damage is done to this organ. Cirrhosis of the liver is the most common ailment of the chronic alcoholics. Excessive drinking affects the nervous system, producing painful nerve inflammation as well as impairing memory and intellectual powers. It also affects sex impulse adversely. Besides drinking affects not only the victim but spouse and children as well, often leading to traumatic experiences and psychosomatic illnesses among the latter.

Drinking the Right Way

If you consider yourself a disciplined person and if you know when to stop as far as alcoholic beverages are concerned, then you may be able to enjoy the relaxation through alcohol by adhering to a few simple rules of intelligent drinking. It is primarily a matter of timing as well as moderation. The time to drink is at the end of a taxing workday, not at lunch and not after dinner. American Medical Association suggests the following five rules:

1. **Set Reasonable Limits for Yourself.**
   Do not exceed a predetermined number of drinks on a given occasion, and stick to your decision. No more than two beers or two cocktails a day is a reasonable limit.

2. **Learn to Say No**
   When you have reached the sensible limit you have set for yourself, politely but firmly refuse to exceed it, no matter who puts pressure on you.

3. **Drink Slowly**
   Do not gulp down a drink. Choose your drinks wisely for their flavor, not their "kick", and enjoy the taste of each sip.

4. **Dilute Your Drinks**
   If you prefer cocktails to beer, try to have long drinks. Instead of drinking your gin or whisky straight, drink it diluted with a mixer such as tonic, water or soda water, in a tall glass.

5. **Do Not Drink on Your Own**
   Make it a point to confine your drinking only to social gatherings, and never drink alone. The urge to relax yourself at the end of a hard day with an alcoholic beverage can be well satisfied with a cup of coffee or a soft drink over a television program or with good book to read.

Statistics Don't Lie

- 11 million Americans are hooked on alcohol.
- 76 million have an alcoholic in their family.
- Every year alcohol claims 100,000 lives in the United States of America.

(Courtesy: Modern Maturity, February-March 1992)

SMOKING

Relaxing?

The commercial advertisements for cigarettes in the newspapers, bill-boards, and elsewhere would have us believe that cigarette smoking is associated with a sense of pleasant relaxation. It is not unusual to see many executives, office workers, and others to light up one cigarette after another during the course of their busy work and stressful situations. It is claimed in their favor that they use cigarettes to reduce uncomfortable feelings—anxiety, tension, boredom, anger, fear, etc.,—in the same way others turn to chemical tranquilizers.

But, does cigarette smoking really induce relaxation in a person under stress? Unfortunately, no! As the cigarette is lit, the smoker invariably inhales the smoke which goes to the lungs, and his/her pulse count goes up anywhere from 5 to 15 beats, indicating an increase in his/her blood pressure. In fact, the cigarette, instead of bringing relaxation, has brought additional stress to the heart—although the smoker may have the psychological impression that it has helped him/her to relax!

The tobacco smoke, whether it is from cigarettes, cigars, or pipes, contains many different substances, among them the three dangerous chemicals: tar, nicotine, and carbon monoxide. The effects of these chemicals on heart and lungs of the smoker have been known to be highly detrimental. The smoke in the tobacco paves the way for cough, bronchitis, emphysema, and increases the risk of lung cancer and heart attack.

Viewed from any angle the evidence points out that cigarette smoking contributes only negatively to the physical and psychological well-being of the smoker. Reaching for a cigarette under stressful situations does more harm than any good and tends to start the vicious cycle of cigarette addiction, with all the attendant trauma of any drug addiction. In a preventive and balanced health management program it is worthwhile for you to pay attention to the warning of the United States Surgeon General that cigarette smoking is dangerous to your health. A wise executive does not go against sensible warnings based on medically verified facts.

Statistics Don't Lie

- 434,000 deaths occur each year due to cigarette smoking and tobacco abuse in the United States of America.

HOBBIES

Hobbies are activities carried on for pleasure. Few executives and professionals realize the importance of having hobbies in their life. Many seem to think that it is a waste of time and energy which they would rather spend at the office desk. What these people have not experienced is the enrichment of their lives obtained from a hobby which money can not buy. Since a hobby is taken up by a person on his/her own interest and inclination, it is not burdensome as a career activity. There are no deadlines to meet, no meetings to attend, and no reports to be filed.

The hobby takes your mind off your busy routines and acts as a decompressor on your nervous system. Since the hobby brings you enjoyment, you will be able to return to your office routines with a mind more clear and less stressful. There are creative and non-creative hobbies. Activities like reading, listening to music, etc., are different from carpentry, gardening, etc. No matter which you choose, all hobbies bring you the same benefits—pleasure and relaxation. One can have one or more hobbies depending on his/her available time, interest, and resources. Then again, one can change the hobby at any time, and adopt it again at some other time.

VACATION

Vacation, if properly planned and executed, can serve as stress-breakers for the executive. It offers an ideal opportunity to get away from the routines of a busy executive life and to enjoy the pleasures of a non-scheduled leisure time with spouse and family. You can travel and visit places of interest away from home; or, you can even simply stay at home if you know how to enjoy yourself doing things you always wanted to do but did not have the time before.

An annual vacation of at least two weeks away from home and office is highly recommended to break the monotony of a busy executive life. Vacations must be considered as a part of executive health planning, if not for anything else.

CHAPTER 10

EXECUTIVE PERFORMANCE EVALUATION

"The touchstone of performance evaluation to assess the greatness or smallness of a person is his own past actions".

Thiruvalluvar,
Thirukural (verse 505)

TOPICS
---

1. Need for Performance Evaluation
2. Factors in Performance Evaluation
3. Subjective Bias in Evaluation
4. The Purdue Rating Scale
5. Using Evaluation to Your Advantage
6. Current Trend in Performance Evaluation

NEED FOR PERFORMANCE EVALUATION

Performance evaluation is an integral part of an organizational assessment for all employees including managers and executives. Evaluations are needed for the following purposes:

1. To assess how well the person is carrying out his/her assigned functional responsibilities;
2. To get an idea of the accomplishments of the person;
3. To find the functional weaknesses and strengths of the person relative to the position in which he/she serves;
4. To assess the person's contributions to the goals and objectives of the organization.
5. To have a rational basis for rewards and punishments such as rise in salary, promotions, merit bonus, transfer, and firing.

Performance evaluations, when carried out and used justly and properly, contribute to the well-being of the organization and the morale of the employees. However, if improperly done, they could undermine the morale of the employees and affect the health of the organization.

FACTORS IN PERFORMANCE EVALUATION

The main factors considered in any performance evaluation are those related to the job functions. Since the job functions of executives and professionals vary from position to position, it is not a fair system that tries to evaluate all the executives with one standardized criteria. Personal, behavioral, and achievement factors must be integrated in any evaluation in a meaningful manner.

The important factors generally targeted for assessment for the executives are:

Intellectual
Emotional
Administrative:
    leadership
    planning
    funds-handling
Capacity
Initiative
Enthusiasm

Accomplishments
Personal relations:
    with bosses
    with subordinates
    with peers
    with the public
Contribution to the organization
Social responsibility
Team work

For jobs of special nature and specific objectives, evaluation criteria should be drawn beforehand.

SUBJECTIVE BIAS OF EVALUATION

Job performance evaluation is not an objective or intellectual process. Most of the factors of evaluation are not amenable for direct measurement but are subject to the bias of the evaluator. A fair-minded evaluation is therefore necessary on the part of the evaluator to make the process as objective as possible and to keep personal bias and prejudice away from the evaluation as far as possible.

Also, the so-called level of performance is a nebulous concept, rated from 'unsatisfactory' at one end to 'exceptional' at the other. In order to quantify the assessment in meaningful terms a rating scale becomes necessary which can be used by two or more people evaluating the same person. An averaging of the rating though numbers becomes possible. However, it should be kept in mind that the rating scale is purely arbitrary in nature and in its range of numbers. Different organizations may use different values. Rating scales on a 5-point system suitably devised for each factor of assessment are widely used. The evaluator assigns a full point from 1 to 5 for each factor as objectively as he/she could.

One such rating scale is the Purdue Rating Scale for Administrators and Executives by H. H. Remmers and R. L. Hobson which is given below. If more than one person evaluates, the rating scores for each item will be averaged.

THE PURDUE RATING SCALE FOR ADMINISTRATORS AND EXECUTIVES

Instructions: You are asked to rate your administrator on the following scale. Your ratings will be anonymous—the administrator will never know how you personally appraised him; he will receive only the average responses of all those who rate him. Read the items carefully. Decide which of the five possibilities best describes your administrator. Place the number corresponding to your choice in the blank at the right.

Name of person being rated _____

I. INTELLECTUAL BALANCE

1. Possesses general knowledge:
   (5) Very broad (4) Fairly broad (3) Limited (2) Very
   limited (1) Lacking .... _____ 1

2. Possesses specific knowledge in his own field:
   (5) Up-to-date (4) Good (3) Fair (2) Poor (1) Lacking _____ 2

II. EMOTIONAL BALANCE

3. Is emotionally poised and calm:
   (5) Always (4) Usually (3) Sometimes (2) Seldom
   (1) Never .... _____ 3

4. Has adequate self-confidence:
   (5) Always (4) Usually (3) sometimes (2) Seldom
   (1) Never .... _____ 4

5. Is concerned with his own personal problems:
   (5) Never (4) seldom (3) Sometimes (2) Usually
   (1) Always .... _____ 5

6. Welcomes differences in viewpoint:
   (5) Always (4) Usually (3) Sometimes (2) Seldom
   (1) Never .... _____ 6

III. ADMINISTRATIVE LEADERSHIP

7. Welds staff into a unit with clearly recognized goals:
   (5) Exceptionally well (4) Very well (3) Quite well
   (2) Poorly (1) Very poorly .... _____ 7

8. Uses democratic procedures wherever possible:
   (5) Always (4) Usually (3) Sometimes (2) Seldom
   (1) Never . . . . _____ 8

9. Inspires subordinates to independent creative work:
   (5) Always (4) Sometimes (3) Seldom (2) Never
   (1) Makes creative work repulsive. . . . . _____ 9

IV. ADMINISTRATIVE PLANNING

10. Makes plan carefully and adequately:
    (5) Always (4) Usually (3) Sometimes (2) Seldom
    (1) Never . . . . _____ 10

11. Is alert to recognize or devise useful innovations:
    (5) Always (4) Usually (3) Sometimes (2) Seldom
    (1) Never . . . . _____ 11

12. Understands the objectives and interrelationships of his entire work:
    (5) Exceptionally well (4) Very Well (3) Quite well
    (2) Poorly (1) Very poorly . . . . _____ 12

13. Does a good job of systematizing and coordinating units of work:
    (5) Always (4) Usually (3) Sometimes (2) Seldom
    (1) Never . . . . _____ 13

14. Has knowledge of pertinent details of his subordinates' work:
    (5) Very good (4) Good (3) Fair (2) Poor (1) Not at all _____ 14

V. USE OF FUNDS

15. Employs as capable personnel as possible:
    (5) Always (4) Usually (3) Sometimes (2) Seldom
    (1) Never . . . . _____ 15

16. Selects equipment wisely:
    (5) Always (4) Usually (3) Sometimes (2) Seldom
    (1) Never . . . . _____ 16

17. Makes effective effort to obtain funds for self-improvement of subordinates:
    (5) Always (4) Usually (3) Sometimes (2) Seldom
    (1) Never . . . . _____ 17

VI. CAPACITY FOR WORK

18. Works hard:
    (5) Always (4) Usually (3) Sometimes (2) Seldom
    (1) Never . . . . ____ 18

19. Welcomes additional responsibilities:
    (5) Always (4) Usually (3) Sometimes (2) Seldom
    (1) Never . . . . ____ 19

20. Meets emergencies in his work competently:
    (5) Always (4) Usually (3) Sometimes (2) Seldom
    (1) Never . . . . ____ 20

VII. ACCOMPLISHMENT

21. Conducts his work as expeditiously as possible:
    (5) Always (4) Usually (3) Sometimes (2) Seldom
    (1) Never . . . . ____ 21

22. The essential work of his organization gets done on time:
    (5) Always (4) Usually (3) Sometimes (2) Seldom
    (1) Never . . . . ____ 22

23. The important work of his organization is completed:
    (5) All of it (4) Most (3) Some (2) Little (1) None . . . ____ 23

VIII. RELATIONS WITH SUBORDINATES

24. Compliments and thanks his subordinates appropriately and sincerely:
    (5) Very frequently (4) Quite frequently (3) Sometimes
    (2) Seldom (1) Often criticizes negatively. . . . . ____ 24

25. Is available to counsel and assist subordinates:
    (5) Sufficiently (4) Almost sufficiently (3) sometimes
    (2) Seldom (1) Never . . . . ____ 25

26. Recognizes and rewards meritorious achievements of his subordinates:
    (5) Always (4) Usually (3) Sometimes (2) Seldom
    (1) Never . . . . ____ 26

27. Possesses insight into the problems encountered by his subordinates:
    (5) Complete (4) Much (3) Some (2) Little (1) None . . ____ 27

28. Is honest and dependable in dealings with subordinates:
    (5) Always (4) Usually (3) Sometimes (2) Seldom
    (1) Never .... _____ 28

29. Displays unwarranted favoritism to some subordinates:
    (5) Never (4) Seldom (3) Sometimes (2) Often
    (1) Continuously .... _____ 29

30. Appropriates ideas and work of subordinates to improve his own
    standing:
    (5) Never (4) Seldom (3) Sometimes (2) Often
    (1) Continuously .... _____ 30

31. Does everything possible, consistent with a subordinate's ability
    and achievement to advance him:
    (5) Always (4) Usually (3) Seldom (2) Never
    (1) Curbs advancement .... _____ 31

32. Is just and considerate in discharging subordinates:
    (5) Always (4) Usually (3) Sometimes (2) Seldom
    (1) Never .... _____ 32

33. The general morale of his staff:
    (5) Exceptionally high (4) Good (3) Fair (2) Poor
    (1) Very poor.................................. _____ 33

IX. PUBLIC RELATIONS

34. Promotes public relations:
    (5) Actively good (4) Fair (3) Poor (2) Not at all
    (1) Actively bad............................... _____ 34

X. SOCIAL RESPONSIBILITY

35. Attempts to orient his work to the welfare of society at large:
    (5) Exceptionally well (4) Well (3) Fairly well
    (2) Indifferently (1) Poorly..................... _____ 35

36. Team work: conforms to the purposes and plans of the organiza-
    tion which he serves: does not seek unfair advantage for his unit:
    (5) Always (4) Usually (3) Sometimes (2) Seldom
    (1) Never .... _____ 36

    *** Courtesy: The Purdue Research Foundation
                    Purdue University, Lafayette, Indiana, U.S.A.

USING EVALUATION TO YOUR ADVANTAGE

It is common practice with most organizations to give a copy of the evaluation report in its final form to the person evaluated in what is called as a "review session" by the immediate boss. The idea is to let the person evaluated know what his/her functional weaknesses and strengths and also the level of performance in the present position are. If the evaluated does not agree, this is the right time to contradict and present evidences in writing in support of his/her own assessment on the counts contradicted.

Of course, the evaluation report goes into the personal file of the executive and becomes a part of the employment cum performance history of the person. The boss can use it for or against the evaluated person in support of his/her decision to give rise, promotion, etc., or to deny them.

Good or bad, what can you do with your evaluation report? In fact, you can do many things. First thing to do is to learn to look at your report objectively without becoming emotional. The report shows you how you and your performance are seen by others. Your strength lies in those areas rated high, and your weakness in areas rated low. You can start working on improving in your weak areas for the next report period. If you are deficient in special skills for a better job performance, you must consider taking special courses, attending seminars, and even going back to school in the evenings or full-time.

Sometimes it may be appropriate to ask for a transfer to another division if you think you can contribute more to the organization. This step is valid only at the lower level executive positions.

If you are totally dissatisfied with your evaluation report in spite of your best efforts at job performance or if you think that there is no more room for vertical mobility you can seriously consider seeking a new position outside of the organization. This step is appropriate only after you have exhausted all the potentials for growth with your present employer.

In general, evaluation reports serve as periodic feedbacks which can help the employer and the executive to move towards common goals.

CURRENT TREND IN PERFORMANCE EVALUATION

R & R Retreat

The current system of rating and ranking (R & R) executives and other employees from the point of view of individual performance has become a point of severe controversy in many leading corporations and other organizations. Greater emphasis is now placed on the ability to play as a team mate rather than as a boss or subordinate. Of course, individual ability has its place in units where research, fundamental or applied, is the focus. Even there it is no longer the case of an isolated scientist doing all the research work for an organization. Even leadership as a distinct individual characteristic has its effectiveness in the ability of the person to be a part of the team and not in the alienation.

Every organization has its purpose and goals, and it is the responsibility of every one working for it to understand them and try to consciously contribute to that end. Moving as a team is the only logical solution. Group success is individual success and vice versa when played as a team. To have and to inspire team spirit in others is the highest virtue of an executive, the hallmark of leadership.

REFERENCES

1. Thiruvalluvar, "Thirukural", Saiva Siddhanta Publishing society, Tirunelveli, Tamil Nadu, India, 1956.
2. Robert R. Blake and Jane S. Moulton, "Executive Achievement", McGraw Hill Book Co., New York 1986.
3. S. A. Swami, "Self-Excellence", Minibook Publishing Co., Montgomery, WV, 1987.
4. Auren Uris, "Developing Your Executive skills", McGraw Hill Book Co., New York, 1955.
5. Aren Uris, "The Executive Deskbook", Van Nostrand Reinhold Company, New York, 1970.
6. James F. Bender, "The Technique of Executive Leadership", McGraw Hill Book Co., New York, 1950.
7. Edward C. Bursk, Editor, "How to Increase Executive Effectiveness", Harvard, University Press, Cambridge, Mass., 1953.
8. Joseph D. Edwards, "Executives: Making Them Click", University Press, New York, 1956.
9. Myles L. Mace, "The Growth and Development of Executives", Harvard University, Boston, Mass., 1950.
10. Frederic R. Wickert and Dalton E. Farland, Editors, "Measuring Executive Effectiveness", Appleton-Century-Crofts, New York, NY, 1967.
11. Qass Aquarius, "The Corporate Prince—A Handbook of Administrative Tactics", Van Nostrand Reinhold Co., New York, 1971.
12. Richard H. Buskirk, "Modern Management and Machiavelli", Cahner Publishing Co., Boston, Mass., 1974.

13. Machiavelli, "The Prince and Other Works", Packard and Co., Chicago, IL, 1941.
14. Maxwell Maltz, "Psycho-cybernetics", Simon & Schuster, Inc., New York, 1960.
15. Kenneth R. Pelletier, "Mind As Healer Mind As Slayer", Delacarte, Press, 1977.
16. Harry Levinson, "Executive Stress", Harper Row Publishers, New York, 1970.
17. Steven Berglas, "The Success Syndrome", Plenum Press, New York, 1986.
18. Jeffrey Lynn Speller, "Executives in Crisis", Jossey-Bass Publishers, San Francisco, CA., 1989.
19. Joseph McKendrick, editor, "Executive Excellence", Administrative Management Society, 2360 Maryland Rd., Willow Grove, PA., 1984.
20. Lorne C. Plunkett & Robert Fournier, "Participative Management", John Wiley & Sons, Inc., New York, 1991.
21. Robert Kreitner, "Management," Houghton Mifflin Co., Boston, 1986.
22. George Mazzei, "Moving Up," Poseidon Press, New York, 1984.
23. David A. West and Glenn L. Wood, "Personal Financial Management," Houghton Mifflin Co., Boston, 1972.
24. George S. Clason, "The Richest Man in Babylon," Hawthorn Books, Inc., New York, 1955.
25. Kenneth H. Cooper, "Aerobics," M. Evans & Co., New York, 1968.

INDEX

ABOUT THE AUTHOR

Shanmugam A. Swami, born on May 30, 1928 in India, received his formal education in three continents. He holds a bachelor's degree in civil engineering from the University of Madras, India, a master's degree from the University of New South Wales, Sydney, Australia, and a doctorate degree from Purdue University, Lafayette, Indiana, USA.

He has served in the industry, Government, and educational institutions over his long career of 42 years. Currently, he serves as a professor of civil engineering in the West Virginia Institute of Technology since 1968. He is a registered professional engineer.

He is the author of two other books: "Self-Excellence" and "The College Student's Handbook for Better Grades, Job Search, and Career Success". He is a past president of Tamil Nadu Foundation, a non-profit organization, and the Founder-President of Minibook Publishing Co., Montgomery, WV.

Well-versed in behavioral psychology and relaxation techniques, Dr. Swami has organized and presented many public and private seminars on Preventive Stress Management and Goal-Oriented Living.

COLOPHON

DESKBOOK OF
EXECUTIVE EXCELLENCE
AND
STRESS MANAGEMENT

Skills, Tactics & Tips for
Superior Job Performance

A MINIBOOK CLASSIC

This book was designed by the author and produced by Minibook Publishing Co., Montgomery, WV.

The text type is 11 on 13 Times Roman.

The typesetting was done by BookMasters, Inc.

The printing and binding was done by BookCrafters, Inc.